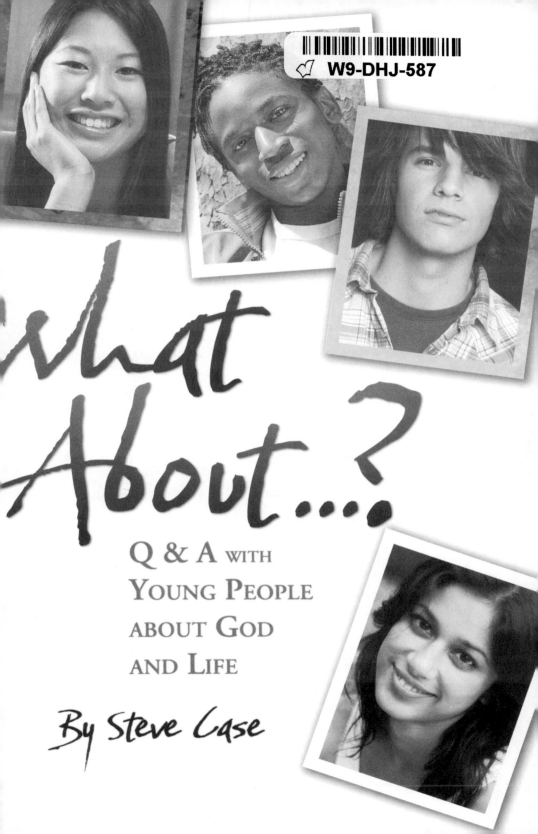

what About....?

Q & A WITH YOUNG PEOPLE ABOUT GOD AND LIFE

By Steve Case

Design by: Palimor Studios
Layout by: Christal Gregerson
Project Manager: Christal Gregerson

Available from:
Advent*Source*
5040 Prescott Avenue
Lincoln, NE 68506
1-800-328-0525
www.adventsource.org

Printed in the United States of America

ISBN# 1-57756-332-8

Dedication

This book is dedicated to the editors of *Insight* magazine over the years.

Michelle Bergmann
Lori Peckham
Dwain Esmond
Tim Lale
Chris Blake

It's been a treat for me to be able to team up with you in ministry!

Table of Contents

What About Giving a Direct Answer?

Question: *I read your column quite a bit, and I think you usually avoid giving direct answers like "Yes" and "No." Are you afraid of offending others? Jesus wasn't. I know you're trying to be cool, but I want direct answers!*

Answer: *Thank you for being honest and direct. Here's my attempt at a direct answer for you.*

First of all, I'm not cool. I used to be, but I lost that about the time I was a teen.

When I respond to people's questions in the *Insight* column, I really do want to provide answers that are Godly, Biblical, honest, and practical. Sounding "cool" is the furthest thing from my mind.

For some questions a simple answer is easy. But most of the questions I receive have more than one possible answer. And when I offer more answers, I'm trying to help you see that life isn't merely a set of simple "Yes" and "No" answers.

Here's an example. A frequent question I receive is "Can I go to the theater?" It would be too simple for me to say "No," because you could go to the theater no matter what I say. And you're getting to the age at which you'll make decisions for yourself.

Maybe you mean "Does God say it's okay or not okay to go to the theater?" I'm not God, but I work for Him. So I look to Scripture for an answer. Since motion pictures were invented about 2,000 years after the Bible was written, there isn't a simple answer in the Bible regarding the theater.

So I end up quoting Philippians 4:8: "Finally, brothers, whatever is true, whatever is noble, whatever is right, whatever is pure, whatever is lovely, whatever is admirable—if anything is excellent or praiseworthy—think about such things."

What wonderful guidelines from God! They aren't specifically about theater attendance, but they certainly apply. Based on these criteria, can/should you go to the theater? That's what you need to decide for yourself, based on what God, your parents, and others have taught you.

Here's how I'd decide. The majority of what plays in theaters doesn't fit Philippians 4:8. So I wouldn't choose to be entertained by that. But some things shown in the theater do jive with Philippians 4:8. So I'd choose to be entertained by those things.

See, a simple "Yes" or "No" for attending the theater doesn't work. (I'm not saying that anybody needs to go to the theater. I'm pointing out that banning all theater attendance isn't consistent with Philippians 4:8.)

It can get more complicated. It's possible never to attend the theater and to watch all kinds of trash on TV or videos/DVDs. Or what if your church rents a theater and conducts evangelistic meetings there? (Some Adventist churches do that.) Should you not go?

I could make things even more complicated. What if the story in Judges 19 was showing in a theater? (It would be terrible!) But God put it in the Bible. Why?

I understand that you wish I'd make answers simple for you. If you were a child, I would. But it's time to grow up and wrestle with more than simple items (see John 7:24).

Most of what you'll face in life isn't simple (unless you ignore a lot of reality). It might not be "cool" to do this, but it's the right thing to do now.

What This is About

I've been involved with young people most of my life. The majority of these youth have grown up with some background regarding God, Church, the Bible, etc. But as a person becomes independent and makes more and more choices, that person's background will influence choices, but it won't determine them. We are not merely computers with a hard drive that somebody has programmed for us. Obviously I believe in the power of choice.

Before making a choice for yourself, it's common to ask for input from others. Young people tend to look to peers for feedback on clothing and hair styles as well as musical preferences, slang and jargon.

But I've found that they are more apt to look to someone older when it comes to topics about God, one's purpose in life, values, and understanding Scripture. It seems that when it comes to these important areas, young people have a sense that peers are still in the search process, too. If adults won't listen or aren't available, young people will turn to peers on these vital topics, but their first choice is adults, usually ones they respect.

This can be intimidating, for young people as well as for adults. Young people don't necessarily want to appear to be stupid or rebellious. Sometimes they need a forum to discuss their issues and take them for a test run. Adults aren't always sure about their answers and may be wrestling with the same questions, too. Is there a safe place to ask questions? Is there a safe person or group of people to dialogue about these things?

I'm grateful that the editors of *Insight* magazine have provided such a place. And I'm humbled that they have asked me to respond to the questions they receive. This weekly publication (www.insightmagazine.org) usually includes a column called "On the Case" in which a young person presents a question and I offer an answer.

This is difficult for me. I'd prefer a dialogue, but all I have is a letter or an email from *Insight*. So, I imagine one of the young people I know to be sitting in my chair across from my computer screen, and I answer as if I were talking to that person I know. Of course, this entire conversation is bathed in prayer. Then I send it to *Insight* and the editors improve it and publish it in the magazine.

I don't find out if the answer hit the mark or not. I've heard from others that a specific answer was just right for them. I'm sure that sometimes my answer is "a misser" (a term my wife uses for something that clearly misses the mark). I can only pray that the Holy Spirit will continue to take the responses and make them worthwhile, just like the Spirit does with our prayers (see Romans 8:26).

I certainly don't claim to know it all or even know much of anything. Because my understanding continues to deepen, my perspectives change with time. Use the questions and answers in this book to start a discussion with others or to think through things by yourself.

I'm a Seventh-day Adventist youth pastor. Much of what I share applies to young people in general. Some of it relates specifically to young people in the Seventh-day Adventist Church. Oh, and some adults will find it either helpful (or offensive), too.

The book is a collection of "On the Case" columns from *Insight* magazine over the past few years. Hopefully, having so many Q & A's in one spot will be a helpful resource. My thanks to Advent*Source* and Brad Forbes for publishing this as a gift book for the North American Division Prayer Conference, and a special thanks to those who gave donations to "Involve Youth" to sponsor this endeavor.

My prayer is that you will always feel free to ask questions and seek answers as you walk life's journey with God.

Questions About God

- ◆ Jesus really being God's son?
- ◆ Jesus—Human or Divine?
- ◆ How Many People Will be in Heaven?
- ◆ Natural Disasters Being God's Judgment?
- ◆ the Start of Sin?
- ◆ Satan's Transfer from Heaven to Earth?
- ◆ God Being "Jealous"?
- ◆ the Trinity?
- ◆ Who We Pray To?

What About Jesus really being God's son?

Question: *Can you prove that Jesus is God's Son?*

Answer: *Can I do it to your satisfaction? Let's see.*

This is far more than a passing question. On it hinges your life's purpose, its direction, its destiny. Believing that Jesus is God's Son requires a certain amount of faith, which can be informed with evidence.

From the start Jesus provoked admiration or rejection. Notice the words of the angel Gabriel to Mary found in Luke 1:30-36: "'Don't be frightened, Mary,' the angel told her, 'for God has decided to wonderfully bless you! Very soon now, you will become pregnant and have a baby boy, and you are to name him "Jesus." He shall be very great and shall be called the Son of God. And the Lord God shall give him the throne of his ancestor David. And he shall reign over Israel forever; his Kingdom shall never end!' Mary asked the angel, 'But how can I have a baby? I am a virgin.' The angel replied, 'The Holy Spirit shall come upon you, and the power of God shall overshadow you; so the baby born to you will be utterly holy—the Son of God'" (TLB).

That's either an incredible miracle or utter foolishness. Either God miraculously placed Jesus in Mary's womb, or else Mary blamed God for an unwanted pregnancy that she wouldn't admit came about any other way than by a miracle.

At the start of Jesus' ministry, the voice of God announced that Jesus was His Son. Mark 1:9-11 records, "At that time Jesus came from Nazareth in Galilee and was baptized by John in the Jordan. As Jesus was coming up out of the water, he saw heaven being torn open and the Spirit descending on him like a dove. And a voice came from heaven: 'You are my Son, whom I love; with you I am well pleased.'"

Not surprisingly, John the Baptist testified that Jesus was the "Son of God" (John 1:34). Then some of John's disciples began following Jesus, claiming He was the Messiah—the One God had promised would save people from sin. And when Nathanael received the call to follow Jesus, he also called Him the "Son of God" (John 1:49).

During Jesus' first miracle—turning water into wine at the wedding feast in Cana—the miraculous sign of Jesus "revealed his glory, and his disciples put their faith in him" (John 2:11).

Evil spirits repeatedly identified Him as the Son of God (Mark 3:11). Not surprisingly, those who felt the benefits of His miracles considered Him to be from God (John 9:30-33). Jesus even claimed it Himself: "I am God's Son" (John 10:36).

The writer C. S. Lewis said that we are faced with one of three options in relating to Jesus, due to the fact that He claimed to be God:

1. Jesus was a liar—since He claimed to be God, either He was, or else He was lying about it.

2. Jesus was a lunatic—a self-deluded Messiah, not necessarily a liar but just crazy.

3. Jesus was God—if neither of the first two is true, then Jesus was indeed who He claimed to be—God!

If either of the first two possibilities is true, it calls for a rejection of Jesus. If the third possibility is reality, our response should be worship.

People can provide various facts that seem to indicate that Jesus was or wasn't divine. But another way to consider your question is how you have come to know Jesus for yourself. If you don't know Him personally, you may need to experience Him a number of times for your faith to grow, like the disciples. Or, you may need only one experience, like the Roman centurion (Mark 15:39). But if you go on the word of others without experiencing Him yourself, you miss the point.

John wrote, "Jesus did many other miraculous signs in the presence of his disciples, which are not recorded in this book. But these are written that you may believe that Jesus is the Christ, the Son of God, and that by believing you may have life in his name" (John 20:30, 31).

Until Jesus becomes the Son of God to you, He will be little more than some historical figure. But when Jesus is the Son of God to you, your entire life will be centered on Him.

Not surprisingly, John the Baptist testified that Jesus was the "Son of God." (John 1:34)

What About Jesus—Divine or Human?

"IF YOU ARE THE CHRIST, TELL US PLAINLY," JESUS' ANSWER TELLS US A LOT: "I DID TELL YOU, BUT YOU DO NOT BELIEVE."

(JOHN 10:22-39)

Question: *Was Jesus totally human or totally divine?*

Answer: *This is actually a simple question and can be answered in one word: totally!*

Let's talk about Jesus' totally human portion first. The genealogy of Jesus (see Matthew 1:1-16) goes through a chain of humans, all the way from Abraham and David (which sounds good), but also through Tamar, Rahab, and Bathsheba (which doesn't sound so good).

Luke 2:1-7 says Jesus was born as a baby in an earthy, primitive setting and describes the reality of taxes, Mary and Joseph's trip to Bethlehem, and their lowly accommodations because "there was no room for them in the inn" (verse 7).

The story continues in Luke with shepherds (lowly humans) being the ones who visited this baby. As a continuation of His human development, Mary and Joseph took Jesus to the Temple for the very human firstborn male Jewish rite of circumcision.

Except for Jesus' trip to Jerusalem when He was 12, the rest of His childhood and adolescence is summed up in Luke 2:52: "And Jesus matured, growing up in both body and spirit, blessed by both God and people."*

We can find many more details about Jesus' three years of ministry during His young adulthood. We read of Jesus getting tired, even exhausted, being hungry, angry, sorrowful, and eventually beaten and killed by other humans. In fact, He hung on a cross between two other humans.

So was Jesus human? Totally!

The second portion of your question asks if Jesus was totally divine. Notice that Jesus' genealogy recorded in Luke 3:23-38 traces His ancestry back to God!

Although Jesus was indeed born in a stable, Wise Men from the East came and worshiped Him. Evidently King Herod didn't mistake Jesus as a mere human since he slaughtered so many baby boys in an unsuccessful attempt to eliminate Jesus (see Matthew 2).

And when Jesus went through the Jewish ritual of circumcision, both Anna and Simeon saw Him as divine (see Luke 2:25-38).

Whether it was turning water into wine, healing the sick, casting out demons, raising the dead, or restoring blind people's sight, Jesus' actions were certainly more divine than human.

When the religious leaders said to Jesus straight out, "If you are the Christ, tell us plainly," Jesus' answer tells us a lot: "I did tell you, but you do not believe" (John 10:22-39).

Jesus then referred to His many miracles and asked the religious leaders which miracle caused their desire to stone Him. They replied, "We are not stoning you for any of these, . . . but for blasphemy, because you, a mere man, claim to be God" (verse 33). And after Jesus basically told them again that He was God, they tried to seize Jesus, "but he escaped their grasp" (verse 39).

How tragic—the religious leaders got the very answer they sought. But they rejected the divine because they thought He was only human. However, the pagan Roman centurion on duty during the Crucifixion noted that Jesus was the Son of God (see Matthew 27:54).

So the answer really is that Jesus was totally human and totally divine.

I know that makes Him 200 percent, but when you're God, totally means more than only human. When you're Jesus, totally means more than only divine, too.

In Hebrews 4:14-16 we read, "Now that we know what we have—Jesus, this great High Priest with ready access to God—let's not let it slip through our fingers. We don't have a priest who is out of touch with our reality. He's been through weakness and testing, experienced it all—all but the sin. So let's walk right up to him and get what he is so ready to give. Take the mercy, accept the help."

"We are not stoning you for any of these, . . . but for blasphemy, because you, a mere man, claim to be God." (John 10:39)

What About How Many People Will be in Heaven?

"THERE ARE MANY ROOMS IN MY FATHER'S HOME, AND I AM GOING TO PREPARE A PLACE FOR YOU. IF THIS WERE NOT SO, I WOULD TELL YOU PLAINLY. WHEN EVERYTHING IS READY, I WILL COME AND GET YOU, SO THAT YOU WILL ALWAYS BE WITH ME WHERE I AM."

(JOHN 14:2, 3, NLT)

Question: *How many people can heaven hold?*

Answer: *Lots of people!*

When I was a small child, our family of five lived in a three-bedroom house. My parents shared one room. My oldest sister had a room to herself (she was the oldest, you see!). And my other sister, who was the second born but still older than I, shared a room with me. I think I could have used more space, but that was all I knew.

As I got older and much more mature—about the age of 5—my parents decided that maybe the girls should be in one room, and the boy should be in a separate room. So my sisters shared a room, and I got a room all to myself. It was amazing how quickly I

8

filled up the new space, since I didn't have to share a room. That was probably when I realized that I "needed" the extra space.

But that all came to an end when my younger sister was born, and my parents moved her crib into my room! I thought the garage would've been a better place for her. Anyway, I got to learn how to share all over again!

My sisters and I played kickball in our front yard. As I got older and much more mature—as an adult—I've had the opportunity to visit that childhood house and its yard. It doesn't seem possible that we played games in the postage-stamp-sized yard. It was so small. Yet I don't remember us ever kicking the ball into the busy street.

You asked about heaven. How large is it? Who will be there? Who won't? What will we do? What won't we do? What will Sabbath be like? What will the food taste like? Will we play basketball?

One of the most common verses people turn to when considering heaven is a misreading of 1 Corinthians 2:9: "As it is written: 'Eye has not seen, nor ear heard, nor have entered into the heart of man the things which God has prepared for those who love Him'" (NKJV).*

This gets explained or paraphrased as, "We have absolutely no idea of what God has in store for us in heaven!" What gets implied is that it's sooo good, that it's beyond our limited, human conception, which may be true! But the very next verse reads, "But God has revealed them to us through His Spirit" (1 Corinthians 2:10, NKJV).

That makes me think that if you have God's Spirit—the Holy Spirit— you will have an idea of what heaven is like! That's just the opposite of having absolutely no idea.

So what's heaven like? How much space is there? How many people can heaven hold?

Several years ago a Christian band called Audio Adrenaline came up with a song about what heaven will be like. Maybe God's Spirit revealed it to them. The lyrics go like this:

"Come, and go with me
to my Father's house.
It's a big, big house,
with lots and lots of room,
A big, big table,
with lots and lots of food,
A big, big yard,
where we can play football
A big, big house,
it's my Father's house."

I like the lyrics to the song, and I like the music, too. I have many fond memories of singing this song at youth retreats and feeling the anticipation of being in heaven with tons of teens, lots of room, food, football, and more. It sounds like heaven to me!

But where did Audio Adrenaline come up with this idea? Are they prophets passing on a message from God's Spirit to us? Actually, I think they're simply paraphrasing Scripture. Here are two passages that I think they may be paraphrasing:

"There are many rooms in my Father's home, and I am going to prepare a place for you. If this were not so, I would tell you plainly. When everything is ready, I will come and get you, so that you will always be with me where I am" (John 14:2, 3, NLT). This is what Jesus said!

"I saw a vast crowd, too great to count, from every nation and tribe and people and language, standing in front of the throne and before the Lamb. They were clothed in white and held palm branches in their hands. And they were shouting with a mighty shout, 'Salvation comes from our God on the throne and from the Lamb!'" (Revelation 7:9, 10, NLT).

In the beginning of Revelation 7 is the listing of the "144,000 who were sealed from all the tribes of Israel." Some people think that heaven holds only 144,000 people. I think the number is symbolic, not literal. Even if it were literal, Revelation 7:9 says "a vast crowd, too great to count, from every nation . . ." go into heaven.

So how big is heaven? How many people can it hold? Since God created the universe, the issues of size and space aren't even issues for Him. Since He is the "Alpha and the Omega, the First and the Last, the Beginning and the End" (Revelation 22:13, NLT), time isn't an issue for Him, either.

During my early childhood years, time and space were issues for me. They still are. But those boundaries are nonexistent for God. There is plenty of room for all who want to be in heaven. According to Revelation 22:17, "The Spirit and the bride say, 'Come.' Let each one who hears them say, 'Come.' Let the thirsty ones come—anyone who wants to. Let them come and drink the water of life without charge" (NLT).

For God, space isn't a problem. The issue for God is whether or not we will choose to be with Him. God's desire all along has been to hang with us; some say "to fellowship together."

When you say, "Yes" to God, He's got all the time in the world and all the room in the universe for you!

"Salvation comes from our God on the throne and from the Lamb!" (Revelation 7:9, 10, NLT)

What About All the Suffering and Pain?

"YOU MUST NOT EAT FROM THE TREE OF THE KNOWLEDGE OF GOOD AND EVIL, FOR WHEN YOU EAT OF IT YOU WILL SURELY DIE."

(GENESIS 2:17)

Question: *Why doesn't God do something about all the suffering and pain around us?*

Answer: *Your question is as old as this earth's history. The best answer I've discovered still doesn't bring suffering and pain to an end until Jesus returns. In the meantime, I need faith to trust that Jesus will put a stop to all suffering and pain eventually.*

Suffering and pain come in many forms—rejection from somebody important to you, physical injuries from accidents or attacks, abuse, war, terrorism, disabilities, death.

Why doesn't God do something? Well, here's what God did before it began: He warned Adam and Eve about what would happen as a result of living apart from Him. In Genesis 2:17 God said, "You must not eat from the tree of the knowledge of good and evil, for when you eat of it you will surely die."

After both Adam and Eve chose their own way instead of God's, suffering and pain began on this earth. The blissful couple went from the Garden of Eden to life outside of the ideal (see Genesis 3:23), which included pain (see Genesis 3:16, 17). And in the very next chapter—Genesis 4—the first murder on this planet is recorded.

Right now we're living between the beginning and the end of suffering and pain. And until the new earth begins, God is doing the following three things about suffering and pain:

1. He identifies with those who are suffering and in pain. In the parable of the sheep and the goats (see Matthew 25:31-46), Jesus explained that ministry to "the least of these" is ministry to Him. And failure to respond or minister to those who suffer is a failure to respond to Jesus.

   If you are suffering and feel pain, Jesus identifies with you. He knows suffering and pain—firsthand (see Hebrews 4:15; Matthew 26:75; Mark 15:15; Matthew 27:46).

2. God has chosen to relieve suffering and pain by ministering through us. You and I are the avenues for God to do something about the suffering and pain we see on this planet. When we ask God, "Why don't You do something about all of the suffering and pain?" we can expect that He'll ask us the same question, since He's equipped us to do something about it (see Ephesians 4:12).

   Do something about suffering and pain where you are (see Matthew 25:34-40).

3. God has taken the results of sin on this planet—suffering and pain—and has transformed them into instruments to reach people with His good news of salvation. Paul wrote that there's no

comparison between our sufferings and what God has prepared for us (see Romans 8:18). This is the guy who was struck blind so he could see Jesus for who He was (see Acts 9:1-9).

It was Paul who also wrote, "I want to know Christ and the power of his resurrection and the fellowship of sharing in his sufferings" (Philippians 3:10).

Suffering and pain will be with us until God makes everything new. Until then, God identifies with those who suffer, He relieves suffering and pain through you and me, and He becomes more real and the only hope for those who do suffer.

That's what God's doing. What are you doing?

"I want to know Christ and the power of his resurrection and the fellowship of sharing in his sufferings." (Philippians 3:10)

What About Natural Disasters Being God's Judgment?

"I WILL GO DOWN AND SEE IF WHAT THEY HAVE DONE IS AS BAD AS THE OUTCRY THAT HAS REACHED ME."

(GENESIS 18:20, 21)

Question: *Do you think Hurricane Katrina could have been God's judgment on New Orleans, like the fire on Sodom and Gomorrah?*

Answer: *Yes, I think it could have been, but I don't think it actually was. I'm wondering why you think it may have been God's judgment on New Orleans.*

Y*ou can find the story of Sodom and Gomorrah in Genesis 18 and 19. After Abraham hosted the Lord and a couple of angels cloaked in human form, the Lord told Abraham, "I will go down and see if what they have done is as bad as the outcry that has reached me" (Genesis 18:20, 21). That's what I call a "hands-on" type of God!*

15

I'm sure glad I wasn't part of Sodom and Gomorrah, aren't you? But then I read in Romans 1 that God's wrath is being revealed from heaven against all of the godlessness and wickedness of men (verse 18). Could that be you and me?

In Romans 2 Paul writes about those who are followers of God. He says that we are "without excuse," and we're "just as bad" (see verse 1 in various translations). If you can make it all the way through Romans 3, you'll get to the punch line that was probably a memory verse for you years ago—verse 23: "For all have sinned and fall short of the glory of God."

Why aren't more people zapped? The answer is in the same passage, in Romans 2:4: "Don't you realize how patient he [God] is being with you? Or don't you care? Can't you see that he has been waiting all this time without punishing you, to give you time to turn from your sin? His kindness is meant to lead you to repentance" (TLB).

You can count on two things: God is in the saving business—He wants to save everyone. And, for those who don't accept the salvation God offers, things will eventually get even worse than the "natural catastrophes" that we've recently seen. If you want a glimpse of how bad it will get, check out Daniel 12:1; Revelation 14:9-11; and Revelation 9:18-21!

You asked specifically about Hurricane Katrina being a judgment on New Orleans, but after Hurricane Katrina other hurricanes unleashed their fury during the rest of that year's "hurricane season." Was God "punishing" the whole Gulf coast? What about the Caribbean islands and the Yucatán Peninsula of Mexico? And don't leave out the earthquake in Pakistan that killed more than those who died in the 1755 Lisbon earthquake. (Adventists point to the Lisbon earthquake as a sign of the "terrible earthquakes at the end of time.")

When something catastrophic happens, we recognize we're not God. We may turn to God for help or to cast blame or to simply ask Why? Even those who claim not to believe in God seem to blame Him when terrible things happen. I suppose that since God is ultimately "in charge," He gets the blame. He seems to be able to take it, even though things like this will continue—and even get worse—before this whole conflict between good and evil comes to a close.

I want to point out that Jesus doesn't place an immediate cause-and-effect relationship between tragic events and judgments from God. Notice His comments in Luke 13:1-5: "About this time Jesus was informed that Pilate had murdered some people from Galilee as they were sacrificing at the Temple in Jerusalem. 'Do you think those Galileans were worse sinners than other people from Galilee?' he asked. 'Is that why they suffered? Not at all! And you will also perish unless you turn from your evil ways and turn to God. And what about the eighteen men who died when the Tower of Siloam fell on them? Were they the worst sinners in Jerusalem? No, and I tell you again that unless you repent, you will also perish'" (NLT).

Here's my rough paraphrase. Don't think that every tragic death is a direct judgment from God. What counts is whether or not you're committed to God, not how you happen to die.

Until this earth's history comes to an end, there will be both calamity and opportunity to minister God's goodness and glory as Paul said in Romans 8:21-23, "All creation anticipates the day when it will join God's children in glorious freedom from death and decay. For we know that all creation has been groaning as in the pains of childbirth right up to the present time. And even we Christians, although we have the Holy Spirit within us as a foretaste of future glory, also groan to be released from pain and suffering. We, too, wait anxiously for that day when God will give us our full rights as his children, including the new bodies he has promised us" (NLT).

Until then, anticipate the new earth, hand out God's mercy to others, and be thankful that God is a judge who's full of mercy—for you as well as for those who are suffering.

What About the Start of Sin?

I CAN SEE WHY THIS IS CALLED A "LAMENT"—IT'S AGONIZINGLY SAD. HOW COULD THE "MODEL OF PERFECTION, FULL OF WISDOM AND PERFECT IN BEAUTY" BECOME SATAN?

Question: *How did sin originate in Lucifer?*

Answer: *This is a most difficult question to answer! I'm going to give you an answer, but it really doesn't make sense to me.*

What was with Lucifer that got him off track? Revelation 12:7-9 tells us "there was war in heaven. Michael and his angels fought against the dragon, and the dragon and his angels fought back. But he was not strong enough, and they lost their place in heaven. The great dragon was hurled down—that ancient serpent called the devil, or Satan, who leads the whole world astray." But it doesn't say how sin originated in Lucifer.

Two passages in the Old Testament that carry double meanings give clues. They describe a ruler or kingdom but mix it with the characteristics of an older source that has the same spirit.

The first one is Isaiah 14:12-15: "How you have fallen from heaven, O morning star [some translations say "Lucifer," which means morning star], son of the dawn! You have been cast down to the earth, you who once laid low the nations! You said in your heart, 'I will ascend to heaven; I will raise my throne above the stars of God; I will sit enthroned on the mount of assembly, on the utmost heights of the sacred mountain. I will ascend above the tops of the clouds; I will make myself like the Most High.' But you are brought down to the grave, to the depths of the pit." By reading Isaiah 13, you'll find that Isaiah 14 is talking about the country of Babylon. The city's egotistical traits are rooted in Satan.

The second passage is Ezekiel 28:12-15: "Son of man, take up a lament concerning the king of Tyre [notice the spirit of Satan in this "lament"] and say to him: 'This is what the Sovereign Lord says: "You were the model of perfection, full of wisdom and perfect in beauty. You were in Eden, the garden of God; every precious stone adorned you: ruby, topaz and emerald, chrysolite, onyx and jasper, sapphire, turquoise and beryl. Your settings and mountings were made of gold; on the day you were created they were prepared. You were anointed as a guardian cherub, for so I ordained you. You were on the holy mount of God; you walked among the fiery stones. You were blameless in your ways from the day you were created till wickedness was found in you."'"

I can see why this is called a "lament"—it's agonizingly sad. How could the "model of perfection, full of wisdom and perfect in beauty" become Satan?

Perhaps you've seen the same scenario play out with a teenager who was born "with a silver spoon in his mouth." He's intelligent, looks stunning, is part of a great family, is wealthy, cultured, has an incredible attitude, demonstrates leadership, is honest, cool, kool, and kewl—he's all that and more. And then, for no explainable reason, he runs away from home at the age of 17 and lives on the streets of a large city. He gives up so much in exchange for so little! You would never do that if you'd been given his opportunities and talents. You wonder, What got into him? That's the story of the "original sin" in Lucifer. He had it made, but for some unexplainable reason, he wanted to be God.

From a human perspective you will always be the child of your parents, but there's no way that your parents can become your children. You've been given the power to create children of your own. Will you rebel because your parents won't be your children? It just can't happen. Neither could God (THE Creator) be replaced by Satan (a creator).

I don't know how long Lucifer plotted to replace God. I don't know how long it took to spread the discord around heaven before that war broke out. I don't know how Satan thought that he would overpower his own source of life. How crazy!

Neither can I explain some of the selfish, ego-maniacal things that I do—except to blame them on Satan. But I have the resources of heaven to help me—I don't have to choose to be evil/selfish. While I was born with a natural bent to be selfish, Satan wasn't created that way.

I look forward to living in heaven, where I won't have that "natural" bent to be selfish. But apparently I will still be able to choose to be a creative creature in heaven instead of the Creator who replaces God. That's something for all of God's creatures to do—on earth and in heaven.

"I want to know Christ and the power of his resurrection and the fellowship of sharing in his sufferings." (Philippians 3:10)

What About Satan's Transfer from Heaven to Earth?

"FROM NOW ON, YOU AND THE WOMAN WILL BE ENEMIES, AND YOUR OFFSPRING AND HER OFFSPRING WILL BE ENEMIES. HE WILL CRUSH YOUR HEAD, AND YOU WILL STRIKE HIS HEEL."

(GENESIS 3:15)

Question: *Did God simply throw Satan out of heaven, or did He throw Satan to earth? If God threw Satan to earth, why?*

Answer: *I think we'll get more details to this critical story when we get to heaven. For now we have a few verses of Scripture that put together basic elements of the story. Let's look at them.*

In Revelation 12:7-9 we can read about a war: "There was war in heaven. Michael and the angels under his command fought the dragon and his angels. And the dragon lost the battle and was forced out of heaven. This great dragon—the ancient serpent called the

21

Devil, or Satan, the one deceiving the whole world—was thrown down to the earth with all his angels" (NLT).

So God did throw Satan down to the earth as a result of war in heaven. But the reasons for the war aren't given here.

In Genesis 3:1-24 you can read about one of Satan's initial activities on earth. It's a story that we sometimes refer to as "the Fall." It begins with Satan appearing to Eve as a wise serpent, which may be difficult for us to imagine, since we've seen serpents only after God cursed them (see Genesis 3:14). We find out that Satan, the serpent, is a liar. When Jesus lived on earth, He confirmed this fact—He called Satan "the father of lies" (see John 8:44).

God pronounced a curse and a promise after the Fall. Genesis 3:15 says: "From now on, you and the woman will be enemies, and your offspring and her offspring will be enemies. He will crush your head, and you will strike his heel" (NLT).

The battle that took place in heaven has been repeated on earth through the ages following Adam and Eve's choice to believe Satan, the serpent. The end result is injury to God and His people (heel being struck) but a deathblow to Satan and his followers (head being crushed).

For reasons that caused the war in heaven, two passages many turn to are in Ezekiel and Isaiah. Ezekiel 28:12-17 reads: "Son of man, weep for the king of Tyre. Give him this message from the Sovereign Lord: You were the perfection of wisdom and beauty. You were in Eden, the garden of God. Your clothing was adorned with every precious stone—red carnelian, chrysolite, white moonstone, beryl, onyx, jasper, sapphire, turquoise, and emerald—all beautifully crafted for you and set in the finest gold. They were given to you on the day you were created. I ordained and anointed you as the mighty angelic guardian. You had access to the holy mountain of God and walked among the stones of fire. You were blameless in all you did from the day you were created until the day evil was found in you. Your great wealth filled you with violence, and you sinned. So I banished you from the mountain of God. I expelled you, O mighty guardian, from your place among the stones of fire. Your heart was filled with pride because of all your beauty. You corrupted your wisdom for the sake of your splendor. So I threw you to the earth and exposed you to the curious gaze of kings" (NLT).

While the context of this passage is actually a description about the king of Tyre, some of the elements can't be about that king, such as being in the Garden of Eden. Since the king of Tyre receives judgment from God for his ungodly actions, it's easy to see that the power behind the king of Tyre is actually Satan.

People also point to Isaiah 14:12-14 as a passage having to do with Satan and his fall, even though the context is aimed at the king of Babylon. The ego-centrism that God points out in these verses is definitely rooted in Satan.

If you were also wondering about the possibility that if Satan wasn't on the earth, maybe Adam and Eve wouldn't have sinned, well, I haven't come across anything in the Bible that addresses that. However, you can find some terrific details that will help to answer your questions in the book *Patriarchs and Prophets* by Ellen White. The first chapter is called "Why Was Sin Permitted?" In it you'll find some really good background details about this entire story. The second chapter is about "The Creation," followed by the next chapters, "The Temptation and Fall" and "The Plan of Redemption." I strongly recommend that you read these chapters.

This story could be rather depressing if it weren't for the reality that Satan wasn't the only one who came to earth. Jesus did, too. And Jesus continues to be present on earth through the Holy Spirit. Even though we don't have a choice about whether or not we're on this earth, as long as I'm here, I choose to be on God's side, not Satan's. How about you?

What About God Being "Jealous"?

When I hear the word "God" I think of words like love, kindness, gentleness, forgiving. I don't usually think of "jealous."

Question: *The Bible says in some places that God is a "jealous" God. Does that mean that jealousy is okay or that God sins?*

Answer: *Perhaps Exodus 20:5 is the text that comes to mind for most when it comes to God being a "jealous God." Since this is the second of the ten commandments, it's not only in the Bible, but also spoken and written by God Himself (see Exodus 20:1; 24:12)!*

Here's how Exodus 20:3-4a reads from the New International Version:

"You shall not make for yourself an idol in the form of anything in heaven above or

24

on the earth beneath or in the waters below. You shall not bow down to them or worship them; for I, the LORD your God, am a jealous God."

If that isn't enough for you, you can find similar statements in Exodus 34:14; Deuteronomy 4:24; Deuteronomy 5:9; and Deuteronomy 6:15.

Make no mistake about it! God claims to be a jealous God. So, to repeat your question, Is jealousy okay, or Is God sinning?

My initial thoughts are that God is good, but jealousy is bad. When I hear the word "God" I think of words like love, kindness, gentleness, forgiving. I don't usually think of "jealous."

When I hear the word "jealous" I think of words like insecure, selfish, immature, petty. I don't usually think of "God."

Maybe I need to take some corrective steps regarding what I think of "God" or what I think of "jealousy." Maybe you do, too.

I checked out the word "jealous" at Merriam-Webster online (www.m-w.com/dictionary/jealous). Here's what I found: "intolerant of rivalry or unfaithfulness; disposed to suspect rivalry or unfaithfulness."

Does this describe God? Is God intolerant of rivalry or unfaithfulness? Absolutely. In fact, that's the context of the second commandment—not to worship any form of idol; God is a jealous God.

The next part of your question asks, "Is jealousy a sin?" (or is God sinning if He's jealous?)

When I think of the times that it seems like I'm jealous, it's usually when I compare myself with someone else who is better than I am and I wish that we could switch places. I also feel jealous when somebody is getting what I want (maybe *attention:* "Isn't he good-looking?" or *material goods:* "She has a fully-stocked entertainment room in her house!" or *recognition:* "He must be the number one person in the whole school!"). I find that the words jealous, envious, and covetous all blend together into one yucky feeling of inadequacy, pity, anger, and misery.

Let's compare this with the dictionary definition of jealous. Am I feeling intolerant of rivalry or unfaithfulness? I'm feeling the rivalry of someone who is either better than I am or who is getting what I think is mine.

But what about being "intolerant of unfaithfulness"? That's usually in the realm of relationships. If my girl is paying more attention to another guy instead of to me, then I will certainly be jealous because I think she's being unfaithful to me. If I won't let her even say a single word to another male under any circumstances, I may need to grow up some and not be so insecure.

As a married man, there's *no way* that I'd tell my wife that she can spend one night a week with another man. I'd be jealous—intolerant of unfaithfulness! And she feels the same way about me.

Those are obvious examples. But what about if I want to go play basketball with the guys one night a week? Should my wife be "jealous" about that? What if I make it five nights a week with the guys? At what point should my wife be jealous? In relationships, those are the types of things that have to be worked out.

Can we put God in the same category as us when it comes to being jealous? Our tendency is to naturally be suspicious, distrustful, and wrongfully envious of others. God is, well, God! Putting Him into a category with anything else makes Him less than God.

No wonder He told the Israelites not to make idols to worship. God is jealous, and He has the right to be.

Perhaps we should ask if His people ever tested that? Um, the answer is "right away" and "repeatedly." While Moses was still on the mountain, the people worshiped a golden calf. And if you want to see frequent idol-worship, check out 1 Kings 13-22.

When Jesus walked this earth, He gave a similar message about God being jealous. Here's how He said it, "No one can serve two masters. Either he will hate the one and love the other, or he will be devoted to the one and despise the other. You cannot serve both God and money" (Matthew 6:24, NIV).

What about you and me? Is God jealous for us? Are we ever unfaithful to God or do we give other things first place in our lives? Certainly we don't worship idols (unless it's *American Idol*). If you want to put it to the test, compare how much money and how much time you spend on yourself just for fun compared to what you spend on God. I'll make it even more simple: how much time do you spend at church on Sabbath compared to how much time do you spend going out on Saturday night? How much money do you put into the offering (you, not your parents) compared to how much do you spend when you go out on Saturday night?

Does God have a right to be jealous? Do you have other things that are number one to you instead of God?

Take it to heart! God is jealous. He has a right to be. So get serious instead of playing games with God. He's loving, forgiving, kind, compassionate, AND JEALOUS. As Paul wrote in Romans 2:4 (TLB), "Don't you realize how patient he is being with you. Or don't you care? Can't you see that he has been waiting all this time without punishing you to give you time to turn from your sin? His kindness is meant to lead you to repentance."

Does God have a right to be jealous? Do you have other things that are number one to you instead of God?

What About the Trinity?

"CHRIST IS THE VISIBLE IMAGE OF THE INVISIBLE GOD. HE EXISTED BEFORE GOD MADE ANYTHING AT ALL AND IS SUPREME OVER ALL CREATION."

(COLOSSIANS 1:15)

Question: *How can God be three in one?*

Answer: *Let me just go on record saying, "I don't know!"*

I *really don't know, but I have a few ideas. There are parts of Scripture that give some clues. But I need to admit right up front that I have difficulty understanding God. Explaining God as three in one is another step beyond my comprehension. But here's my attempt at trying to explain something we call the Trinity.*

Some people point out common examples of three in one, such as a traffic light. We call it a traffic light (singular) even though there are actually three lights—green, yellow, and red. All three work together as a unit. One isn't better than another—

actually, I usually prefer green—yet each light serves a function. Together they serve a more comprehensive function.

Another example is the properties of water. In its liquid state we know it as water, and we use it for drinking, cleaning, and recreational activities, such as wakeboarding, water balloon fights, rafting, etc. But it also comes in a solid state known as ice. We use water in this form for cooling, recreation, refreshment, etc. But water can also come in a gaseous state that we call vapor or steam. We use it for heat, energy, etc. That's a "three in one" that you don't always think of, unless you're in chemistry class.

An example that makes more sense to me is the cheese, lettuce, and tomato sandwich that my wife makes. I like cheese sandwiches. I sometimes will eat a sandwich with only tomatoes. I haven't tried a lettuce sandwich yet. But there's something special about all three coming together in one sandwich! That's a "three in one" that's making me hungry right now!

What does the Bible have to say about God being three in one? I think that whenever something is bigger or stronger or smarter than we are, we tend to give it godlike status. Kids would classify these as superheroes. In athletics they are called superstars. And, yes, in modeling they are called supermodels.

When kings went to war in Bible times, people often turned to gods to help them overcome their enemy. People have always had gods, such as the sun, rain, earth, rivers, oceans, mountains, even the moon, because they realized that many things in nature were bigger and more powerful than they were. Not surprisingly, when a king overcame another kingdom, the idea came to him that he was a "superking" and probably more of a god than the gods of the defeated people.

God's people were given a very different presentation when it came to the whole god thing. Instead of having lots of gods (and people thought that more was better—sort of like more toys or more money or more food, etc.), the God of the Israelites said, "I'm the only God you need." It was—and is— God's number one message in the Ten Commandments (see Exodus 20:3).

When you read the Old Testament and come across LORD, all capital letters, that's actually the name "Yahweh." Also, the word "Elohim" gets translated as "God" or "god," depending on whether it's referring to Yahweh (God) or some other small, supposed deity (god). The lead-in to the first commandment reads like this: "Then God instructed the people as follows: "I am the Lord your God, who rescued you from slavery in Egypt. Do not worship any other gods besides me" (Exodus 20:1-3, NLT).

Yet Yahweh's people repeatedly worshiped other gods. Sometimes they just followed other people—and their gods—instead of Yahweh, and the results were bad.

When Jesus came as the Messiah, the whole idea of one God named Yahweh got challenged, because Jesus claimed to be Yahweh (John 8:58, 59; 10:33). When Jesus said, "The Father and I are one" (John 10:30, NLT), He was claiming that the one God, Yahweh, was actually two in one—Father and Son. It was a Father-Son relationship in terms of closeness, not in terms of one starting before the other.

John made this concept clear at the beginning of his Gospel. He wrote: "In the beginning the Word already existed. He was with God, and he was God. He was in the beginning with God. He created everything there is. Nothing exists that he didn't make. Life itself was in him, and this life gives light to everyone" (John 1:1-4, NLT). In John 1:14 we read that "the Word" was Jesus.

Paul later wrote, "Christ is the visible image of the invisible God. He existed before God made anything at all and is supreme over all creation" (Colossians 1:15, NLT). So, after finally getting it right that there is only one God (Yahweh), there were all of a sudden two! But the two were one!

People often think of an ideal husband and wife as two being one. God explained it this way at Creation: "Then God said, 'And now we [plural] will make human beings [plural]; they [plural] will be like us [plural] and resemble us [plural]. They will have power over the fish, the birds, and all animals, domestic and wild, large and small.' So God created human beings [plural], making them to be like himself [singular]. He [singular] created them [plural] male and female" (Genesis 1:26, 27, TEV). God seems to be able to understand two being one much better than we ever have!

But God stretches us even more. Before Jesus left earth, He tried to tell His disciples that there was another part of the Godhead. After pointing out that Jesus and God the Father are interchangeable, because the two are like one (John 14:8-11), Jesus introduced the Holy Spirit: "I will ask the Father, and he will give you another Counselor, who will never leave you. He is the Holy Spirit, who leads into all truth. The world at large cannot receive him, because it isn't looking for him and doesn't recognize him. But you do, because he lives with you now and later will be in you. No, I will not abandon you as orphans—I will come to you. In just a little while the world will not see me again, but you will. For I will live again, and you will, too. When I am raised to life again, you will know that I am in my Father, and you are in me, and I am in you" (verses 16-20, NLT).

If you can understand that, you've got it! I get lost in the "I in you, you in Me, I in the Father, the Father in Me, the Father and I in you, and the Spirit is in Me."

Paul seems to use the Father, Jesus, and the Holy Spirit quite easily together. In Romans 5:1-5 Paul wrote about the benefits of trusting God. Among other things he mentions peace with God because of what Jesus has done (verse 1). In addition to the gift of Jesus, God also gives us the Holy Spirit to fill our hearts with God's love (verse 5). Paul also points out that God's love for us also came shining through Jesus' death for us while we were sinners (verse 8).

Romans 8 also uses God (the Father), Christ, and the Holy Spirit throughout the chapter. Paul explains that the Godhead went all out to restore the relationship with us that was broken by sin. God is the initiator. And since He is the one and only God, any sub-god or anti-god is essentially a non-factor (verses 31, 38, 39).

Perhaps when it comes to trying to understand how God can be three in one, we'd get a better idea by first being overwhelmed with God's love for us. With all three demonstrating love in so many ways, it's pretty incredible that God, Jesus, and the Holy Spirit do so much for you and me!

Here's what Paul—and I—wish for you when it comes to understanding God as three in one: "When I think of the wisdom and scope of God's plan, I fall to my knees and pray to the Father, the Creator of everything in heaven and on earth. I pray that from his glorious, unlimited resources he will give you mighty inner strength through his Holy Spirit. And I pray that Christ will be more and more at home in your hearts as you trust in him. May your roots go down deep into the soil of God's marvelous love. And may you have the power to understand, as all God's people should, how wide, how long, how high, and how deep his love really is. May you experience the love of Christ, though it is so great you will never fully understand it. Then you will be filled with the fullness of life and power that comes from God" (Ephesians 3:14-19, NLT).

With all three demonstrating love in so many ways, it's pretty incredible that God, Jesus, and the Holy Spirit do so much for you and me!

What About Who We Pray To?

Question: *If Jesus taught His disciples to pray "Our Father, which art in heaven," why do we usually pray, "Dear Jesus"? Is it okay to pray to Jesus, or should we pray to God the Father? Or does it matter, since they are all God?*

Answer: *Since Jesus and "Our Father" are both part of the Trinity, I don't think it matters if you start your prayer as "Our Father" or "Dear Jesus." For that matter, don't forget the Holy Spirit who "prays for us with groanings that cannot be expressed in words" according to Romans 8:26 (NLT).*

There's something more important than using the right form of addressing

God. It's more important that you actually pray! I'm amazed at how little I pray when you consider that the God of the universe has given me direct access to Him. Why don't I tap into this more, not only for power to live for Him and to also confess where I mess up, but just to be in touch. I use my cell phone all the time, but my connection with God doesn't even have "bad cells" where the connection can be cut off.

An extreme example of NOT addressing God with the correct language is the case of the demoniac. This demon-possessed man took the correct posture of falling down before Him, but his words hardly followed the "Our Father" or "Dear Jesus" examples you mentioned. Notice what the demoniac said in Mark 5:7 (NLT), "He gave a terrible scream, shrieking, 'Why are you bothering me, Jesus, Son of the Most High God? For God's sake, don't torture me!'"

And Jesus went ahead and cleansed the man, driving the demons right out of him. That's why I believe that getting the words right isn't as important as getting some words out!

The few verses before "The Lord's Prayer" indicate the contrast of praying to God the way Jesus taught and what people were doing at the time. "When you pray, don't babble on and on as people of other religions do. They think their prayers are answered only by repeating their words again and again. Don't be like them" (Matthew 6:7-8a, NLT).

It's not a matter of saying it "just right" or of saying it a million times (hoping that one of these times God might hear us). Just say it!

The fact that Jesus started the prayer with "Our Father" reveals that Almighty God, the one that creates and destroys, the one that heavenly beings bend the knee to, the starting and ending point, the source of light and life, etc., etc., etc., is our dad! That's right, we start our prayers with the identifying mark that this is all being done "in house." God is OUR FATHER!!!

I'm not going to go into the whole "I-have-a-distorted-image-of-God-because-my-own-father-was-a-bad-father" thing. If you've had a bad dad, then you know that a good dad is the opposite of that, okay? If God were a bad dad, you and I wouldn't even be around. So let your negative images go, and pray to God as your father. Go ahead and adapt it to "My Father" instead of even "Our Father."

Here's how *The Message* paraphrases Romans 8:15-17, "This resurrection life you received from God is not a timid, grave-tending life. It's adventurously expectant, greeting God with a childlike What's next, Papa?' God's Spirit touches our spirits and confirms who we really are. We know who he is, and we know who we are: Father and children. And we know we are going to get what's coming to us—an unbelievable inheritance! We go through exactly what Christ goes through. If we go through the hard times with him, then we're certainly going to go through the good times with him!"

By the way, the rest of "The Lord's Prayer" (after the "Our Father") deals with the basics regarding God, us, others, and living on this planet. Check it out for yourself in Matthew 6:9-13.

As far as the relationship between "Our Father" and "Dear Jesus" is concerned, read John 14:1-26. You'll find that the disciples didn't understand that relating to one is like relating to the other. Plus, they found out that God would be with them in the form of the Holy Spirit (also referred to as Counselor and Comforter and Teacher and Reminder).

The reality for you and me is that "Our Father" and "Dear Jesus" are both in heaven for us, while the Holy Spirit is on this earth and in our hearts! No wonder Paul could say, "With God on our side like this, how can we lose?" (Check out Romans 8:31-39 for a full version.)

No matter how you address Him, tap into communication with God!

More Questions About God

- ◆ Salvation?

- ◆ Having a Relationship with God?

- ◆ Free Choice?

- ◆ The Difference Between Sinners and Sin?

- ◆ Blasphemy Against the Holy Spirit?

- ◆ When God Lets Me Down?

- ◆ Spending Quiet Time with God?

- ◆ Waiting for God?

- ◆ The Age of Christ's Disciples?

- ◆ The Baptism of the Holy Spirit

What About Salvation?

"IF YOU FORGIVE THOSE WHO SIN AGAINST YOU, YOUR HEAVENLY FATHER WILL FORGIVE YOU. BUT IF YOU REFUSE TO FORGIVE OTHERS, YOUR FATHER WILL NOT FORGIVE YOUR SINS."

(Matthew 6:14,15)

Question: *In some Bible verses it says that all you have to do is believe, and you're saved. But in other verses it says that there are all these things you have to do. Which is it?*

Answer: *Let me see if I can come up with some of the verses you might have read or heard about from others on this topic. Then we'll take a look at the bigger picture to figure this out. Sometimes a single text can be very helpful, but sometimes one isolated text from the Bible doesn't tell the whole story.*

Acts 16:30, 31: *"He then brought them out and asked, 'Sirs, what must I do to be saved?' They replied, 'Believe in the*

Lord Jesus, and you will be saved—you and your household.'"

Romans 10:9: "If you confess with your mouth, 'Jesus is Lord,' and believe in your heart that God raised him from the dead, you will be saved."

2 Chronicles 7:14: "If my people, who are called by my name, will humble themselves and pray and seek my face and turn from their wicked ways, then will I hear from heaven and will forgive their sin and will heal their land."

Matthew 6:14, 15: "If you forgive those who sin against you, your heavenly Father will forgive you. But if you refuse to forgive others, your Father will not forgive your sins" (NLT).

Do these verses in the Bible contradict each other? Is salvation a matter of believing you are forgiven, or is there a list you check off first?

I think that the broader view of belief and salvation has to do with how you relate to God. If you relate to God as a police officer, then you'll take a by-the-book approach. For example, you'll want to know the date and time when you "believed." As long as you do that, legally God has to save you, right? You may want to have photos taken and witnesses on hand so that you can prove your salvation later if you need to.

But if you relate to God as a positive parent instead of a police officer, then you'll take a long-term approach, since it's an ongoing relationship. For example, buying groceries or paying rent to stay in your own house might not enter your mind—that's what your parents do! But what do you have to do to believe that? As their child, that's just the way it is.

Your parents might ask you to vacuum or take out the garbage or do the dishes. You don't have to ask, "Which one of these do I have to do in order to be your child?" Helping around the house just comes with being part of the family.

Even though your parents aren't perfect, the things that they "make you do" are often for your benefit as you become increasingly independent.

Even when you're "on your own," you'll still be their child, and they will still be your parents. The relationship dynamics will change, but you will still be related.

Do you relate to God as someone to make an appointment to be with? Or are you with Him all the time? Do you see Him when He pulls you over like a cop, or is He involved throughout your life like your parents?

If Jesus needs to police you, He can do that. But He wants to have a friendship with you (see Revelation 3:20). In an ongoing relationship, Jesus not only forgives you, but He also cleanses you from sin, and your friendship keeps on going. After all, heaven is not primarily about being in a police speed trap where you try to avoid the cops. Heaven is primarily about being with Jesus, your friend.

If I were limited to one verse to respond to your question, it would be 1 John 1:9: "If we confess our sins to him, he can be depended on to forgive us and to cleanse us from every wrong. [And it is perfectly proper for God to do this for us because Christ died to wash away our sins]" (TLB).

In an ongoing relationship, Jesus not only forgives you, but He also cleanses you from sin, and your friendship keeps on going.

What About Having a Relationship with God?

"THIS IS ETERNAL LIFE: THAT THEY MAY KNOW YOU, THE ONLY TRUE GOD, AND JESUS CHRIST, WHOM YOU HAVE SENT."

(JOHN 17:3)

Question: *I love going to church and learning about God. I'm a Seventh-day Adventist by birth, but I'm afraid I don't know how to have a relationship with God. Every time I try to have one, it never seems to work out right—I seem to slip back into sin. I know God is coming soon, and I really want to go to heaven, but I don't know how to have a relationship with Him. Please help me!*

Answer: *This is perhaps my favorite question that any teen has ever asked me!*

It sounds as if you're living on the edge of Jeremiah 29:13, which says, "You will

41

seek me and find me when you seek me with all your heart." The very next verse provides this promise:

"'I will be found by you,' declares the Lord" (Jeremiah 29:14).

When your motivation is strong, of course you'll seek God with all you have. Some people have an incredibly strong motivation to seek God when an emergency gets their attention. They want everything that has to do with God at that moment.

But what happens after the emergency passes? If their interest in God is based only on emergencies, they are sometimes referred to as "foxhole Christians"—people wanting God only when hiding from enemy fire in a foxhole.

You've got the right idea when it comes to wanting to have a relationship with God. After all, that's what God wants, too.

Some say that people are restless until they finally get together with God. Others say that each person has a hole inside them that only God can fill. Jesus said it this way, "This is eternal life: that they may know you, the only true God, and Jesus Christ, whom you have sent" (John17:3).

How can you have a relationship with God? Start with what you already know about relationships. How do you have a relationship with another person? You spend time with that person. Sometimes you'll do things together that you like to do, and sometimes you'll do things together that the other person wants to do. If you don't share interests, you probably won't want to spend too much time together.

When your interests match up, or if your interests change to the other person's interests, then you'll enjoy doing those things of interest together. For example, some people like to spend their time playing sports, shopping, playing video games, just talking on the phone, or e-mailing or text messaging. Some like to go to events, such as a sports event, a concert, or a program at church. And then there's just hanging out together (or whatever teens call it where you live).

One of the things that makes a relationship with God difficult is that you can't see God face-to-face like you can your friends. If one of your friends moves a long way away, it's usually more difficult to maintain that relationship, especially if you operate on the out-of-sight-out-of-mind principle.

Paul wrote about our relationship with God this way, "We can see and understand only a little about God now, as if we were peering at his reflection in a poor mirror; but someday we are going to see him in his completeness, face to face. Now all that I know is hazy and blurred, but then I will see everything clearly, just as clearly as God sees into my heart right now" (1 Corinthians 13:12, TLB).

Don't expect a relationship with an invisible God to be effortless, but don't expect it to be impossible, either. Because this relationship is with God, you can have contact with Him at any time and in any place. You can't have that with a human friend. Plus, God is also seeking a relationship with you. So you don't have to worry about whether or not He likes you, thinks you're weird, or if He wants a relationship with you.

John said it this way, "We know how much God loves us because we have felt his love and because we believe him when he tells us that he loves us dearly. God is love, and anyone who lives in love is living with God and God is living in him. And as we live with Christ, our love grows more perfect and complete; so we will not be ashamed and embarrassed at the day of judgment, but can face him with confidence and joy, because he loves us and we love him too. . . . So you see, our love for him comes as a result of his loving us first" (1 John 4:16-19, TLB). You can read Paul's version in Romans 8:31-39. I like *The Living Bible's* paraphrase of this passage.

Not everyone is the same, so I can't give you a simple equation for having a relationship with God. Here's what's worked for some different people I know:

Person 1: spends 15 to 30 minutes each morning before school reading a portion of the Bible, then praying.

Person 2: spends 5 to 10 minutes praying after crawling into bed at night.

Person 3: listens to Christian music "all the time."

Person 4: goes on a mission trip at least once a year.

Person 5: actively participates in things at church; not just a spectator who says, "That was boring."

Person 6: did the required service hours for the Adventist school credit, but kept on doing service activities simply to serve.

Person 7: leads a small group Bible study once a week and is always looking for contact with God to be able to lead the Bible study.

Person 8: turns every situation into a prayer, whether it's out loud or silent; always seems to be experimenting with new ways to pray.

Person 9: reads one to two chapters from the Bible and then journals a response.

Person 10: does random acts of kindness (often anonymously) and has joined a small support group to live out one's Christianity.

Person 11: memorizes portions of the Sermon on the Mount (Matthew 5-7), then looks for ways to live it right now.

Person 12: participates in every religious youth event possible.

I notice three basic keys that these people tap into in order to have a living relationship with God. I suggest that you find ways to make these keys central to your life so you can have a relationship with God:

1. Get input from God. Get it from the Bible, from listening to God in prayer, in small groups, in church, in Sabbath school, at retreats, etc.

2. Give input to God. Pray, journal, meditate, and get actively involved in discussions with others about God—discussions, not debates or fights.

3. Serve others. Serving others provides you with the unique experience of being God's hands, feet, eyes, and ears to/for others.

Plus, you get to see and sense Jesus in others, too! Serving others greatly enhances your relationship with God.

How has God communicated to you? Look around and check out God's activity in the world (see Psalm 19 and Romans 1:19, 20).

And here's how God started His final message to His people: "Long ago God spoke in many different ways to our fathers, through the prophets [in visions, dreams, and even face to face], telling them little by little about his plans. But now in these days he has spoken to us through his Son to whom he has given everything, and through whom he made the world and everything there is. God's Son shines out with God's glory, and all that God's Son is and does marks him as God" (Hebrews 1:1-3, TLB).

You—and everyone else—have a tremendous advantage when it comes to having a relationship with God. We have God's Word, which has been recorded for centuries! We have the story of Jesus, who was God walking right on earth! Plus, we have the Holy Spirit, who has been given to us "to fill our hearts with his love" (Romans 5:5, TLB).

Although God is invisible, there's really no reason to miss Him. Excuses are flimsy, especially since God is wanting to have a relationship with you, too. Keep going for it. You can be friends with God!

We have the Holy Spirit, who has been given to us "to fill our hearts with his love."

(Romans 5:5, TLB)

What About Free Choice?

"FOR YOU HAVE

BEEN CALLED TO

LIVE IN

FREEDOM—NOT

FREEDOM TO

SATISFY YOUR

SINFUL NATURE,

BUT FREEDOM TO

SERVE ONE

ANOTHER IN

LOVE."

(Galatians 5:13)

Question: *If God gives us free choice, why will He destroy people who don't choose Him?*

Answer: *At first glance it might appear that God doesn't give us free choice at all. If the options are choose God or die, that's not much of a choice, is it?*

Free choice seems to predate the creation of our world. It goes clear back to Lucifer in heaven. Revelation 12 provides several verses on this topic:

"Then there was war in heaven. Michael and his angels under his command fought the dragon and his angels. And the dragon lost the battle and was forced out of heaven. This great dragon—the ancient serpent called the Devil, or Satan, the one deceiving the whole world—was thrown down to the earth with all his angels" (Revelation 12:7-9, NLT).

Let me paraphrase and comment on these few verses. When you think of the word "war," free choice probably doesn't come to mind. It's more like "force" and "might" to the point of either death or surrender. Sometimes people go to war for the cause of free choice, but during the war it's about who can beat whom.

The war in heaven was about who would be God. The dragon (Lucifer, Satan, the Devil, the Serpent, etc.) lost. As a result, God forced him out of heaven. If I were God, I would have ended it all for Satan right then. But because God puts a premium on free choice, He kept Satan alive and free to make his case, so the rest of creation could have the choice to either follow God or Satan.

Besides being deceptive, notice what else Satan— this created being who was given free choice and continues to exist by God's power—has been doing.

"The accuser has been thrown down to earth—the one who accused our brothers and sisters before our God day and night. . . . The Devil has come down to you in great anger, and he knows that he has little time" (Revelation 12:10, 12, NLT).

That sounds pretty serious to me. The concept of "free choice" doesn't come to mind when I read about an "accuser" who works full-time. Mix that with some anger, no, "great anger," and you have a recipe for coercion, destruction, attacks—anything but "free choice."

When people hear the term "free choice," they sometimes think of making choices without consequences. For example, if I have the freedom of choice to kill my sister when she makes me mad, does that mean there are no consequences for me? Or if I have the freedom to steal $1,000 from a bank, are there no consequences?

Let's put this example into the life of a typical teen. If I have the freedom to talk behind the back of my friend, is there no consequence? If I have the freedom to surf the Internet and fill my mind with pornography, is there no consequence? If I have the freedom to move from pornography to having sex with someone, are there any consequences?

In the United States we have many freedoms to be able to choose all kinds of things that many people never get to choose. But that doesn't mean we're also free of consequences. I've seen broken hearts, broken lives, broken relationships, broken toys, broken schools, broken families, broken trust, broken churches, broken plans, and broken hopes. When you have the freedom to choose, there are consequences that come with that privilege.

Because we're born with a sinful nature, our natural selfishness keeps pushing us to make choices with bad consequences. We seem totally helpless to stop hurting ourselves in this way. It's like we've been born on Satan's side, and we can't get away from him—we don't seem to have any choice.

Does this sound like what Paul was talking about in Titus 3:3? "Once we, too, were foolish and disobedient. We were misled by others and became slaves to many wicked desires and evil pleasures. Our lives were full of evil and envy. We hated others, and they hated us."

Does that sound like freedom of choice to you? It sounds like a rat race down the tubes to me. Paul continues in Titus 3:4-7: "But then God our Savior showed us his kindness and love. He saved us, not because of the good things we did, but because of his mercy. He washed away our sins and gave us a new life through the Holy Spirit. He generously poured out the Spirit upon us because of what Jesus Christ our Savior did. He declared us not guilty because of his great kindness. And now we know that we will inherit eternal life."

You can find similar messages that Paul wrote in Colossians 3:1-10; Romans 6:4-14; and Romans 6:20-23. You can also read all of Galatians 5, which can be summarized in verse 13: "For you have been called to live in freedom—not freedom to satisfy your sinful nature, but freedom to serve one another in love."

Because God gave me a fresh start with the freedom to choose something besides just being selfish all the time, I chose Him. It was great. But I found that I continued to face many choices—would I stay with God, or would I slip back into total selfishness? Finally I just told God,

"I'm choosing You for the next five years, and after that we'll see whether or not I want to do that again." But it didn't work. Within a day I was again faced with whether or not I'd be choosing God in my life.

With Satan, it's not like that at all. All you have to do is choose him once, and he's willing to take away all your choices from that point on. Some people actually prefer that (if you can believe it!). But with God, you will continue to choose, virtually every day of your life. Your power of choice is crucial to God.

It's like this—we aren't born with the freedom of choice. Out of God's goodness and kindness He gave back to us the freedom of choice. So your freedom of choice is a gift from God, the Creator of life. What you choose to do with it will determine your consequences. You can choose life with God, or you can go back to your no-choice life of being dominated by Satan. There isn't a middle ground of just being yourself. Either way, God will honor your choice.

Some say, "With the options we face, there really isn't much of a choice—choose God and live, or don't choose God and die."

I agree that the choice seems obvious. But the truth is, Satan gives you no choice; God does. So what will you do with the choice God gives you?

"With the options we face, there really isn't much of a choice—choose God and live, or don't choose God and die."

What About the Difference Between Sinners and Sin?

Question: *I hear all kinds of things about Christians being judgmental and close-minded. How should we balance loving the sinner and hating the sin? I don't want to seem like I accept things that I know are wrong, but I don't want people to think that I don't love them, either.*

Answer: *Bravo to you! You want to be accepting and love people without being judgmental like close-minded Christians. And what a "balancing act" it is to love the sinner and yet hate the sin.*

The first text that comes to my mind when I read your question is one I've often heard others quote—1 Peter 3:15-16 (TEV),

"Be ready at all times to answer anyone who asks you to explain the hope you have in you, but do it with gentleness and respect."

"Gentleness" and "respect" often get associated with "loving," although I think they have more to do with kindness than love. Being "ready to give an answer" indicates that you have given some advance thought to what you believe and why you believe it.

When you know these things, it's much easier to give an answer that is factual and personal, such as, "I would rather not come to your party since it sounds like it's just a gathering to get drunk and I've chosen to be filled with the Holy Spirit rather than with booze (see Ephesians 5:18)."

But if you're not sure that drinking a little is really wrong or that being included with friends is more important than taking a stand, you might wiggle out of taking a stand and say something like, "Thanks man, I'll see if I can be there," and then not show up and say something came up.

You can try other topics besides drinking. One that often pushes people to extremes is homosexuality. Christians opposed to homosexuality point to texts that seem to say it's a bad thing (typical texts cited include Romans 1:27-28 and Jude 7). Our family went to a Christian youth leaders convention. Outside was a group of back-woods-looking people with big signs denouncing homosexuality. Because they were making a strong, public stand, many of the Christians at the convention (including my daughter), took them on in a debate. I saw some people engaged in the discussion because of the topic, while others took a stand based more on how people were going about the topic (not just "what you say" but also "how you say it").

Another hot topic in America has been America's involvement in Iraq. Christians don't necessarily agree on this one—some believing that evil must be held in check or destroyed (like when the Israelites wiped out groups of people when entering Canaan—remember the conquest of Jericho [see Joshua 6]). Other Christians quote Romans 12:21, "Overcome evil with good." Another branch of this debate is how to relate to Muslims when you're a Christian. The Crusades pitted these two religious groups against each other. Some think it will be repeated. How do you make a decision (a "judgment") on these topics without being "judgmental" of others?

Occasionally a street-corner preacher on a soap box wins a convert, but usually it's just bad press to witness in this manner. Popular youth speaker Rob Bell made a DVD presentation called "Bullhorn." In it, a guy with a bullhorn tries to shout his message to people in order to convert them. In the words of Pastor Bell, "Hey bullhorn guy, it's not working."

How can you love the sinner and hate the sin? Only by having the love of God. The most familiar verse in the entire Bible demonstrates this, "For God so loved the world that He gave His only begotten Son, that whoever believes in Him should not perish, but have everlasting life" (John 3:16, NKJV).

A characteristic of Jesus was that he went after people to help them, not to hurt or condemn them. The next verse of John 3 makes that plain. "For God did not send his Son into the world to be its judge, but to be its savior" (John 3:17, TEV).

I wish that I could say that was all there is to it. But the next few verses of John 3 point out a reality that you won't be able to escape, and it very much relates to your question. Let's continue, "Whoever believes in the Son is not judged; but whoever does not believe has already been judged, because he has not believed in God's only Son. This is how the judgment works; the light has come into the world, but people love the darkness rather than the light, because their deeds are evil. Anyone who does evil things hates the light, because he does not want his evil deeds to be shown up. But whoever does what is true comes to the light in order that the light may show that what he did was in obedience to God" (John 3:18-21, TEV).

Here's my paraphrase: Good and God go together. Bad seeks to avoid good and God. You can't have it both ways.

Good and gentle Jesus hated the sin and loved the sinners. Those who were known as bad people flocked to him. Those who were considered good on the outside are the ones who did him in.

How is it with you? Do those known as "bad people" want to be around you (because of your goodness, not because you're a chameleon)? If that's the case, don't be surprised if those considered good on the outside will pass negative judgment on you (see Luke 7:38-39; Matthew 9:9-13).

It is possible to love and accept people without loving or accepting what they do. Family members do it all the time. So do friends. Just because you don't want to smoke with somebody doesn't mean you reject everything about them. Just because one of your friends has a problem with gossip doesn't mean that you drop them immediately. And just because you have a tendency to lie to cover yourself doesn't mean that you get kicked out of your family or your friends will never accept you again. Hopefully your family and friends will work with you on your faults while they love and accept you for being a child of God.

In the same way, love and accept others because they are children of God, not because of their behaviors. Try this approach: "Do not bring sorrow to God's Holy Spirit by the way you live. Remember, he is the one who has identified you as his own, guaranteeing that you will be saved on the day of redemption. Get rid of all bitterness, rage, anger, harsh words, and slander, as well as all types of malicious behavior. Instead, be kind to each other, tenderhearted, forgiving one another, just as God through Christ has forgiven you" (Ephesians 4:30-32, NLT).

And I can't guarantee that everything will be "nice" for you when you do this. Our first text, when taken in context, gives a much broader message. I think it summarizes my response to you. It goes like this: "Who will harm you if you are eager to do what is good? But even if you should suffer for doing what is right, how happy you are! Do not be afraid of anyone, and do not worry. But have reverence for Christ in your hearts, and honor him as Lord. Be ready at all times to answer anyone who asks you to explain the hope you have in you, but do it with gentleness and respect. Keep your conscience clear, so that when you are insulted, those who speak evil of your good conduct as followers of Christ will become ashamed of what they say. For it is better to suffer for doing good, if this should be God's will, than for doing evil" (1 Peter 3:13-17, TEV).

What About Blasphemy Against the Holy Spirit?

"THE

UNPARDONABLE

SIN"—IS WHEN A

PERSON'S

CONSCIENCE HAS

DENIED GOD'S

PROMPTINGS

THROUGH THE

HOLY SPIRIT SO

MANY TIMES THAT

THEY NO LONGER

REGISTER.

Question: *What is "blasphemy against the Holy Spirit"? Why can we blaspheme Jesus and still be forgiven, but we can't blaspheme the Holy Spirit and be forgiven?*

Answer: *The text that most people refer to when mentioning "blasphemy against the Holy Spirit" is Matthew 12:31, 32. Here's how it reads in The Living Bible: "Even blasphemy against me or any other sin can be forgiven—all except one: speaking against the Holy Spirit shall never be forgiven, either in this world or in the world to come".*

T*he answer I've heard from others is that blasphemy against the Holy Spirit—*

sometimes called "the unpardonable sin"—is when a person's conscience has denied God's promptings through the Holy Spirit so many times that they no longer register. You might call it being dead to God. The reason it's not forgiven is that the person no longer even requests forgiveness.

As is often the case, reading these verses in context can provide a more accurate understanding. In one of my Bibles the heading for Matthew 12 is "Opposition to Jesus."

Verses 1-8 tell about the Pharisees complaining to Jesus about the disciples breaking the Sabbath. Jesus concludes the conversation by claiming to be the Lord of the Sabbath—as God, He rules the Sabbath; the Sabbath doesn't rule Him.

Verses 9-14 describe Jesus' healing of a man with a withered hand on Sabbath in a very public manner. Afterward Jesus asked the rhetorical question "Is it OK to do good on the Sabbath?" His enemies didn't answer. The story ends with the Pharisees plotting to kill Jesus.

Verses 15-21 record that Jesus withdrew from the controversy with others who followed Him because they needed healing. Then Jesus healed a demon-possessed blind and mute man, leaving people to wonder if Jesus was the Messiah.

The Pharisees came back into the picture and suggested that Jesus' supernatural power must have come from Beelzebub, the prince of demons!

Jesus didn't withdraw this time. Instead, He took their reasoning to its logical conclusion—if He was from Satan, and He was casting out Satan, then Satan was dividing and conquering himself.

The religious leaders had been blaspheming Jesus, suggesting that He was on the devil's side! They were saying, "You are from hell." What a blasphemous thing to say to God!

Notice how patient Jesus continues to be, after all He's done and all the flack He's received for healing people!

At the Last Supper Jesus explained to His disciples, "There is so much more I want to tell you, but you can't bear it now. When the Spirit of truth comes, he will guide you into all truth. He will not be presenting his own ideas; he will be telling you what he has heard. He will tell you about the future. He will bring me glory by revealing to you whatever he receives from me" (John 16:12-14, NLT).

Here's my paraphrase from combining these two passages: Pharisees, you keep stiff-arming me—to keep me away from you and from so many other people. You even blacken my name and go so far as to say I'm from the devil instead of from God. But in spite all of that, you can still be forgiven! And, after you kill me, you can still be forgiven ("Father, forgive them, for they do not know what they are doing" [Luke 23:34]). And after that, I will still send you the Holy Spirit, who will show you that I really was God. But after that, I will have done everything I can for you. If you keep rejecting me after I send you the Holy Spirit, you simply won't be forgiven. Until then, forgiveness is still possible for you, even after you've killed God!

If you've ignored or rejected God's forgiveness, please, by all means, embrace it right now! It makes all the difference in the world—and in the world to come!

Notice how patient Jesus continues to be, after all He's done and all the flack He's received for healing people!

What About When God Lets Me Down?

SOME PEOPLE HAVE THE IDEA THAT BY BEING FRIENDS WITH GOD AND GIVING YOUR LIFE TO HIM, YOU WON'T HAVE ANY MORE TROUBLES, QUESTIONS, OR MISUNDERSTANDINGS. I HAVEN'T FOUND THAT TO BE THE CASE.

Question: *I pray all the time and I have grown to trust in God. What do I do when I feel like He has let me down?*

Answer: *I would say that you should pray about it! If you pray all the time, then pray about this, too. You wouldn't be the first person to do so. Check this out:*

"*I counted on you, God. Why did you walk out on me? Why am I pacing the floor, wringing my hands over these outrageous people? Give me your lantern and compass, give me a map, so I can find my way to the sacred mountain, to the place of your presence, to enter the place of worship, meet my exuberant God, sing my thanks with a harp, magnificent God, my God.*

"Why are you down in the dumps, dear soul? Why are you crying the blues? Fix my eyes on God—soon I'll be praising again. He puts a smile on my face. He's my God."

That's one of David's Psalms (chapter 43 from *The Message*). Consider it a prayer and tap into any of them. Some of the Psalms are praise prayers, and some are angry ones.

I've gone through my Bible and color-coded them so that I know right where to turn to an expression that matches what my mood is or what I want it to be.

For example, if you're looking for some praise passages, go to Psalm 19, 33, 47, 66, 67, 89, 92, 100, 119, 138, and 145-150. There are others, and parts of some, but here's a good start.

If you're wanting a Psalm of calling out for help, try Psalm 6, 22, 69, 86, 88, or 142.

How about something regarding God's care and protection? Turn to Psalm 12, 23, 31, 41, 46, 56, 91, 121, 127, or 136.

Are you angry? Instead of holding it in and getting an ulcer, or instead of spewing it out on others, dump it on God. That's what David did in Psalm 69 and 109. You'll also find fragments of anger in Psalm 35, 58, 70, 79, 137, and 140.

And two classic Psalms on the topic of forgiveness are Psalm 51 and 103.

Many of the Psalms combine several of these elements or moods, such as Psalm 1, 9, 18, 27, 28, 37, 71, and 138.

Try reading one Psalm a day and come up with your own color codes. They are a great way to continue your relationship with God. Some of them come out of the stories of David found in 1 and 2 Samuel. A concordance will tell you which ones came out of which stories.

Some people have the idea that by being friends with God and giving your life to Him, you won't have any more troubles, questions, or misunderstandings. I haven't found that to be the case.

I do believe that I'm with the Winner and the one who created me and has a purpose for me. But that doesn't mean my life is easy, trouble-free, or in constant communion with God. There are times when God seems to be silent. There are other times when I don't want to talk to Him. It's a dynamic relationship. Sometimes it's the difficult times that actually grow my faith to trust Him based on our relationship to that point, not just on what's happening at the moment.

I'm so glad that you pray all the time. Be sure to include reading Scripture as part of your time with God since you already have some input from God there. Note the types of relationships God has had with others in the Bible. Who are your heroes? With whom do you identify?

And keep on praying! You're right on track!

I'm with the Winner and the one who created me and has a purpose for me.

What About Spending Quiet Time with God?

"YOU MUST TEACH THEM [INSTRUCTIONS AND INPUT FROM GOD] TO YOUR CHILDREN AND TALK ABOUT THEM WHEN YOU ARE AT HOME OR OUT FOR A WALK; AT BEDTIME AND THE FIRST THING IN THE MORNING."

(Deuteronomy 6:7, TLB)

Question: *I'm the only Christian in my home, and I'm finding it hard to spend time reading my Bible and praying. There are so many distractions. Do you have any suggestions for what I can do?*

Answer: *Just this morning my wife told me that she needs at least two more hours each day in order to do everything she feels she needs to do. And that doesn't include additional things she'd like to do but doesn't really need to do.*

Her situation deals more with busyness, though, while yours deals with distractions. Still, the key word for both situations is boundaries. Recently authors *have written books specifically on this topic, because so many people have difficulty setting and maintaining appropriate boundaries.*

For example, some people say to their friends, "I'll always be here for you, no matter what!" Initially they may sound like a dedicated friend. But what if two of their friends want their undivided attention at the same time? There's no way they can "be there" for both of them simultaneously.

Probably when you were younger your parents set boundaries for you, such as when to go to bed, what to eat, maybe even who your friends were or weren't. But now you should be taking on more and more responsibility for making your own decisions, which includes setting your own boundaries.

Since you're the only Christian in your home, obviously you're the one who'll have to set the boundaries for your spiritual input—taking time with God. Remember the advice to the Godly parents in Deuteronomy 6:7: "You must teach them [instructions and input from God] to your children and talk about them when you are at home or out for a walk; at bedtime and the first thing in the morning" (TLB).

Again, you'll have to take responsibility for your spiritual input. You get to grow up faster than others in this area. But others have done it, and so can you!

Consider Samuel, who had special time with God during his childhood (1 Samuel 3:1-21), even though Eli hadn't been successful in getting his own children to relish being with God (1 Samuel 2:12).

You're capable of deciding whether or not you'll spend time with God. It's not just a matter of sliding into it by default. You actually must choose it!

There will always be distractions. Even in the Garden of Eden there were major distractions (see Genesis 2:15, 16 and Genesis 3:1-7). Sometimes the distractions are even good things (see Luke 10:38-42). If you're looking for a distraction-free environment, you need a new perspective.

Sometimes you can't change your environment. But you can be changed (2 Corinthians 5:17). And when you're changed, your environment will no longer control you. You'll actually be a positive influence on your environment instead!

Again, you'll have to take responsibility for your spiritual input. You get to grow up faster than others in this area. But others have done it, and so can you!

What About Waiting for God?

Question: *Why is it that when I need something really badly, and it's something good, and God knows I need it—He waits so long to give it to me?*

Answer: *Why does God wait so long? Several possible scenarios come to mind:*

1. God doesn't really care about speed or timing.

2. God thinks it's better for you to wait.

3. God would like to give you what you asked for faster, but for some reason He isn't able to pull it off.

4. God operates on a different timetable than you do.

5. Other: _____

A few Bible texts come to mind, also. Check these out:

"I will answer them before they even call to me. While they are still talking to me about their needs, I will go ahead and answer their prayers!" (Isaiah 65:24, NLT).

"Ask, and you will receive; seek, and you will find; knock, and the door will be opened to you. For everyone who asks will receive, and anyone who seeks will find, and the door will be opened to those who knock. Would any of you who are fathers give your son a stone when he asks for bread? Or would you give him a snake when he asks for a fish? As bad as you are, you know how to give good things to your children. How much more, then, will your Father in heaven give good things to those who ask him!" (Matthew 7:7-11, TEV).

"This is what I want you to do: Ask the Father for whatever is in keeping with the things I've revealed to you. Ask in my name, according to my will, and he'll most certainly give it to you. Your joy will be a river overflowing its banks!" (John 16:23, 24, Message).

"You want what you don't have, so you scheme and kill to get it. You are jealous for what others have, and you can't possess it, so you fight and quarrel to take it away from them. And yet the reason you don't have what you want is that you don't ask God for it. And even when you do ask, you don't get it because your whole motive is wrong—you want only what will give you pleasure" (James 4:2, 3, NLT).

When I consider your question and then read these passages of Scripture, I'm left wondering why praying doesn't seem to work for you. Then I realize that it doesn't always seem to work for me, either. I don't always get what I want from God when I want it—money, friends, power, prestige—all kinds of good things.

My prayer life reveals how shallow and selfish I am. But after God listens to my requests, He's eager to change my heart and desires so that I start praying for the things He desires for me.

If you don't have a clue what those things might be for you, try praying the Sermon on the Mount (Matthew 5-7). Try praying these portions of each of these three chapters:

Matthew 5:3-12—ask God to make you poor, sad, humble, eager to do what's right, full of mercy for others, pure on the inside, a peacemaker, and then to be treated unfairly to the point of being persecuted. If that isn't enough, jump to verses 44-48.

Matthew 6:9-13—ask God just to answer these items.

Matthew 7:12—start doing it as much and as fast as you can.

Praying this way won't be easy. Few worthwhile things are. But I'm discovering that prayer includes asking God for what we want; but it's more about asking God to change us for good than merely to satisfy us for the short term.

My prayer life reveals how shallow and selfish I am. But after God listens to my requests, He's eager to change my heart and desires so that I start praying for the things He desires for me.

What About the Age of Christ's Disciples?

WITH A FRESH
MENTION OF
YOUNG DISCIPLES,
I'M HOPEFUL
THAT YOUNG
PEOPLE WILL
IDENTIFY WITH
THEM NOW
RATHER THAN
PUTTING OFF
FOLLOWING JESUS
UNTIL THEY ARE
OLDER.

Question: *Does anyone know how old the disciples were when they started to follow Jesus?*

Answer: *No.*

As a child, I remember looking at the artwork in some Bible story books my parents often read to me. Those paintings had old-looking disciples with long, gray or even white beards. I didn't know the age of the disciples, but I was sure they were old, maybe the age of my grandparents. But then, when I was only four or five years of age, even 20-year-olds seemed old to me!

Occasionally I've heard religious speakers make a brief reference to the age of the disciples, indicating that they were much younger than most of us usually think of them. It's usually a passing remark with an encouragement for young people to follow Jesus when they are young, sort of like Solomon's advice in Ecclesiastes 12:1.

As a youth pastor, I like to hear statements that include young people because too often it seems like young people need to wait until they are older, maybe even much older, before they can do something for God. With a fresh mention of young disciples, I'm hopeful that young people will identify with them now rather than putting off following Jesus until they are older.

But what does the Bible say about the age of the disciples? How old were they when they started to follow Jesus?

The Bible doesn't say anything about their age, so we don't know.

Then why do people sometimes refer to the disciples as being towards the younger end of the age span when Jesus called them?

The life span wasn't as long in the days of Jesus as it is in developed countries today. According to some encyclopedias, the average lifespan in North America today is about 80 years, compared to half of that as recently as the 1800s (see http://en.wikipedia.org/wiki/Maximum_life_span).

Jesus started His public ministry, including the calling of His disciples, when he was about 30 years of age (see Luke 3:23). We don't know it for sure, but we sort of expect that the disciples who followed Jesus were probably younger than He was. But does younger mean 29 years old or 19 years old? I don't think that anyone seriously thinks of Jesus picking five-year-old boys to be His disciples at that time!

When Jesus called Peter and Andrew, James and John to leave their fishing nets and to follow Him (Mark 1:16-20), we realize that they were old enough to be fishermen. Some think that someone in their 20s or 30s would be a good age for casting nets into the sea and then pulling them out with a collection of fish. You don't think of older men with sagging backs doing that type of work. When James and John followed Jesus, they left their father and the other workers in their father's boat, leaving us to wonder if they weren't old enough yet to have the family business. Were they doing their internship or apprenticeship?

It seems clear that the disciples of Jesus weren't college educated, or maybe not even high school educated. Evidently they were old enough to be able to step out on their own. Peter was married (see Matthew 8:14), but that probably occurred earlier than it does for many who have an extended education today.

According to Ellen White (see *The Desire of Ages*, page 292), John was the youngest disciple. We don't know how old the disciples were when they died. Traditional stories indicate that they died as martyrs, prior to "old age." The one exception was John. When they tried to kill him by putting him into a pot of boiling oil, he didn't burn. So, to remove him from influencing more people, they banished him to the deserted island of Patmos.

But it was on Patmos that John wrote the book of Revelation. Many scholars date John's writing of the book of Revelation at 96 AD. That is 69 years after the disciples were called by Jesus! How old could John, the youngest disciple and the brother of James, have been when he was called by Jesus? I can see why some suggest that he could easily have been a teenager!

Let me say it one more time, the Bible doesn't say how old the disciples were when Jesus called them. How old were you when you started to follow Jesus? If you haven't made a decision to follow Jesus, both He and I invite you to do so now. It's one of those things in which "the sooner the better" definitely applies. Who knows, you may end up writing another book of Revelation or simply being a revelation of Jesus Christ!

What About the Baptism of the Holy Spirit?

Question: *What does it mean to be baptized by the Holy Spirit?*

Answer: *In Acts 19 you can find a story about Paul's first visit to the city of Ephesus. Paul found some "disciples," followers of God, and he asked them, "'Did you receive the Holy Spirit when you believed?' They answered, 'No, we have not even heard that there is a Holy Spirit'" (verse 2).*

The rest of the story is found in verses three to six. "So Paul asked, 'Then what baptism did you receive?' 'John's baptism,' they replied. Paul said, 'John's baptism was a baptism of repentance. He told the people to believe in the one coming after *him, that is, in Jesus.' On hearing this, they were baptized into the name of the Lord Jesus. When Paul placed his hands on them, the Holy Spirit came on them, and they spoke in tongues and prophesied."*

People reference this story when they get re-baptized after going away from God and then returning. Actually, there's no indication that the people in Ephesus had left God. They simply found out more about God and wanted to be brought up to speed. They'd accepted the baptism that John the Baptist had preached (see Mark 1:4). But Paul told them about the One John had predicted—Jesus. So they were baptized into the name of "Jesus."

Following this second baptism—into the name of "Jesus"—Paul placed his hands on them, and the Holy Spirit came on them. By now you're probably wondering, Is this what people mean when they refer to the baptism of the Holy Spirit?

John the Baptist prophesied, "I baptize you with water. But one more powerful than I will come, the thongs of whose sandals I am not worthy to untie. He will baptize you with the Holy Spirit and with fire" (Luke 3:16).

The night before His death Jesus told His disciples, "I will ask the Father, and he will give you another Counselor to be with you forever— the Spirit of truth. The world cannot accept him, because it neither sees him nor knows him. But you know him, for he lives with you and will be in you" (John 14:16, 17).

A few verses later Jesus continued, "If anyone loves me, he will obey my teaching. My Father will love him, and we will come to him and make our home with him" (verse 23). Jesus' statement leads me to believe that the Trinity (Father, Son, and Holy Spirit) is a package deal. When you get One, you get all Three! The baptism of the Holy Spirit is the same as the baptism of Jesus, and it includes the Father as well (see Ephesians 2:18).

Explaining the reality of God's promise, Paul put it this way: "You also were included in Christ when you heard the word of truth, the gospel of your salvation. Having believed, you were marked in him with a seal, the promised Holy Spirit, who is a deposit guaranteeing our inheritance until the redemption of those who are God's possession" (Ephesians 1:13, 14).

I think people tend to attribute supernatural thrusts to "the baptism of the Holy Spirit." But the Holy Spirit is a gift that's available to everyone who accepts Jesus into one's life. At that point the Holy Spirit immediately begins to change a person's character through the process of developing the fruits of the Spirit in their life (see Galatians 5:22, 23). The Holy Spirit also immediately provides a person with spiritual gifts to minister the way Jesus did.

As always, God, Jesus, and the Holy Spirit are readily available to us. Sometimes our awareness or receptivity is limited, and sometimes we're wide open to them. If you don't sense the Holy Spirit's active presence in your life, pray for Jesus to come into your life this instant, then live completely for Him, trusting the Holy Spirit to change you and minister to others through you. Then John the Baptist's prediction will be true for you—Jesus will have baptized you with the Holy Spirit and with fire.

The Holy Spirit is a gift that's available to everyone who accepts Jesus into one's life.

Questions About Faith

- GRACE?

- FORGIVENESS?

- BEING SURE I'M SAVED?

- GROWING UP WITH JESUS BUT NOT LOVING HIM?

- GETTING SAVED BY THE TIME JESUS RETURNS?

- CREATION AND EVOLUTION?

- WHEN PRAYER DOESN'T WORK?

- FEELING CLOSE TO GOD?

- SPIRITUAL WARFARE?

- GETTING BAPTIZED?

- SPIRITUAL GROWTH?

- REVIVAL?

What About Grace?

HOW CAN YOUNG PEOPLE BELIEVE IN BOTH LEGALISM AND GRACE AT THE SAME TIME?

Question: *How do you balance legalism and grace?*

Answer: *This might be the most difficult question I've ever received!*

In the late 1980s, Seventh-day Adventist youth in North America answered survey questions about a bunch of things. Their answers became a study called Valuegenesis. I was a member of the research team, and the results that took us all by surprise were teens' answers to a set of questions about salvation. They were asked if they thought salvation resulted from keeping the law (legalism) or from grace.

Some responses showed an emphasis on legalism (keeping the law), and other responses indicated a bent toward grace (God's gift). The research team then raised the question, How can young people believe in both legalism and grace at the same time?

Let's start by describing these two concepts. Legalism has to do with a strict, literal, or excessive conformity to the law. It's like going 56 miles per hour in a 55-mile-per-hour zone and getting a ticket for it. Grace is a gift you don't deserve. It's like getting stopped for going 85 in a 35-mile-per-hour zone and getting a warning instead of being thrown in jail!

How do you balance excessive conformity to the law with giving people what they don't deserve? It's not a matter of mixing black paint with white paint and ending up with a balanced gray paint. Legalism and grace just don't mix. It's not a matter of oil and water not mixing either. At least those two substances stay apart from each other. Legalism and grace conflict with each other.

Here's the classic Bible text for grace: "For it is by grace you have been saved, through faith—and this not from yourselves, it is the gift of God—not by works, so that no one can boast" (Ephesians 2:8, 9).

I think the reason people try to balance legalism with grace is that it seems that grace is just too risky and dangerous. Grace is bountiful and gushing. Legalism is limited and confining. They just don't balance.

Another factor is that sometimes we don't want to accept a gift. As we're growing up, our parents teach us to be responsible and to take care of ourselves, so we become independent of their life-sustaining gifts. But independence isn't a good thing when it comes to God. Not taking Him up on His life-sustaining gift is fatal.

Some people throw God's laws out the window and claim to live only by grace. But God's laws aren't bad. It's our poor performance in living the law in a legalistic way that's bad. Let me explain by putting it in a mathematical equation like this:

Law = good
Sin = bad
Grace = super-good

Here's how these three relate to each other:

Sin > law (Romans 7:13)
Grace > sin (Romans 5:20)

Putting these in a progressive equation from least powerful to most powerful looks like this:

Law < Sin < Grace

Legalism focuses on a good thing, the law. But the law isn't strong enough to deal with sin. Grace is God's gift that overpowers sin. So why would you even want to "balance" legalism with grace? How do you balance the two when sin is in the middle? Go for grace all the way!

By the way, Adventist teens were recently tested again to see if they still tended toward legalism or grace. This time results showed a noticeable shift towards grace. I think teens are now heading in the right direction instead of getting pulled opposite ways.

Cling to grace. Because of it, rejoice and live in gratitude! You'll find this idea presented in great detail in Romans 1-8, particularly in the New Living Translation.

Cling to grace. Because of it, rejoice and live in gratitude!

What About Forgiveness?

"IF YOU FORGIVEN THOSE WHO SIN AGAINST YOU, YOUR HEAVENLY FATHER WILL FORGIVE YOU. BUT IF YOU REFUSE TO FORGIVE OTHERS, YOUR FATHER WILL NOT FORGIVE YOUR SINS."

(MATTHEW 6:14-15, NLT)

Question: *How do I forgive someone that's really hurt me? Do I have to forgive them in order for God to forgive me?*

Answer: *You've asked a really tough question, and one that affects most everyone, and some more than others! And then you bring God into the topic, too! Good for you!*

T*he answer to your first question depends on the answer to the second question, so let's look at the second question first—Do I have to forgive others in order for God to forgive me?*

If you've ever prayed The Lord's Prayer, have you noticed what's right in the middle of that prayer? It goes like this: "And forgive us our sins, just as we have forgiven those who have sinned against us"

(Matthew 6:12, NLT). If God answers your prayer, God will be just as forgiving with you as you are with others. Is that what you want?

That possibility leads me to misquote Jesus when I pray. I prefer to say, "And forgive me my sins, *much more* than I have forgiven those who have sinned against me." But that's not what the Bible says.

If that isn't direct enough, right after The Lord's Prayer, Jesus said, "If you forgive those who sin against you, your heavenly Father will forgive you. But if you refuse to forgive others, your Father will not forgive your sins," (Matthew 6:14-15, NLT).

How's that for a direct answer? Do you have to forgive others in order for God to forgive you? YES!

The answer is true, but it might not be helpful, unless you consider another story or two from Jesus.

One of these can be found in Matthew 18:23-35. It's called the story of the unforgiving debtor. A king had a servant who owed him more than he could ever repay. Out of mercy, the king forgave him. The forgiven debtor happened to come across a fellow servant who owed him a small amount of money. But the forgiven debtor, the one who had received an unfathomable amount of mercy, passed along no mercy to his fellow-servant. When the king found out, he had the unmerciful, unforgiving servant thrown into jail. The story concludes with these words from Jesus, "That's what my heavenly Father will do to you if you refuse to forgive your brothers and sisters in your heart" (Matthew 18:35, NLT).

Perhaps the most critical insight from this story is where your focus is. If you focus on others who owe you something (such as somebody who has hurt you), they will always be in your debt. But if your focus is on God who has forgiven you of far more hurt than any amount somebody else can hurt you, you'll just pass along the mercy. A focus on Jesus makes you seek justice for others except for when it comes to something others have done against you—then you go for mercy instead of justice.

Your first question was, "How do I forgive someone who has really hurt me?" I don't think you can "just do it" or grit your teeth and just spit out the words, "You're forgiven, you _____, _____, _____!"

When somebody has hurt you, that hurt often changes into anger, resentment, revenge, and bitterness. Sometimes it turns to a victimization that leaves you in pain, pity, and limping like a handicapped person. Either way you're a mess! Commanding you to forgive at that moment isn't likely to engender much openness on your part. Here's what I recommend:

PRAY! Dump the whole thing on God. If you keep it inside, it will make you rot. If you spew it back on the person who hurt you, you'll probably make things worse. If you dump it on somebody else, you'll either be gossiping or recruiting an army to attack back. That's why I say you should pray at a time like this.

If you don't know what to say to God at times like this, try Psalm 109 (the whole Psalm). If that isn't enough, go on to Psalm 69:18-29. In fact, keep reading through the Psalms—there are praise ones as well as pouting ones, and others, too.

After lancing your hurt, ask God for the *gift* of forgiveness. That's right, it's a *gift* from God. It's not something that you work up. It's not something you can purchase or even practice. It's a gift from God, so you'll need to go directly to the source in order to ever forgive somebody who has hurt you. Feeling guilty because you know you should forgive the person but you don't want to won't make you forgiving either. You simply go to God and ask God for the *gift* of forgiveness.

If that sounds too easy, here's the hard part. The thing the person did that hurt you is something you need to hand over to God. Just like a quarterback hands off the football to a running back, you need to hand off the injustice and hurt to God. That means you have to let it go! And that's the hard part!

Why is that hard? It means that you have no right to get the person back for how they wronged you! Will you turn that over to God? God is the one who said, "I will take vengeance; I will repay those who deserve it" (Deuteronomy 32:35, NLT). (also quoted in Romans 12:19 and Hebrews 10:30). God can get somebody back much worse than you ever could. But there's always the chance that God will just forgive them (like He has forgiven you).

Jonah found that troubling. When God didn't destroy the people of Nineveh, Jonah cried out, "I knew that you were a gracious and compassionate God, slow to get angry and filled with unfailing love. I knew how easily you could cancel your plans for destroying these people" (Jonah 4:2, NLT).

It seems as though this angry prophet had forgotten that this gracious, compassionate, and forgiving God was the same One who saved him in chapter one of Jonah!

When we're hurting, we're more apt to feel sorry for ourselves and point out what's wrong with the other person than to recall the forgiveness that God has already given to us!

Some people are likely to point out that it would be good to go directly to the person who hurt you and to confront them and give them a chance to ask for forgiveness. Or you might consult with a trusted Christian friend to help you maneuver through the sensitive situation. I suppose that can be helpful. But that often seems to me sort of like putting a tiny band aid on a series of machete slashes across your entire gut!

What you need is the gift of forgiveness! Only God can give that to you. The other person might not even know they have hurt you. Or if they do know it, they aren't likely to ask for forgiveness. When God has given you the gift, you can pass it along whether the other person asks for it or not (see Matthew 5:23-24)!

When Jesus had His feet anointed by a notoriously sinful woman at a special dinner, the host (who was a Pharisee) found himself offended that the woman did this AND that Jesus didn't get rid of the woman. Jesus clarified his intentions with this analogy: a man loaned two people some money; one received $500 and the other one received $50, and the man forgave both of them their debts. Which one will love him more? The Pharisee spoke the obvious, "I suppose the one for whom he cancelled the larger debt."

In case anyone missed the point, Jesus summarized it as, "Those who have been forgiven little show only a little bit of love; but those who have been forgiven much will show much love" (see Luke 7:36-50 for the whole story).

If you have a hard time forgiving others, maybe it's because you haven't received much forgiveness yourself. Go to the source of forgiveness—God—and confess your mess-ups, dumping all your garbage so you can receive His gift of forgiveness. Then you will be able to show love and forgiveness because of what you have received from Him to pass on. That's much better than hanging onto the hurt and letting it continue to destroy you!

"Those who have been forgiven little show only a little bit of love; but those who have been forgiven much will show much love."

What About Being Sure I'm Saved?

IF YOU DOUBT YOUR SALVATION, IT MIGHT BE A NUDGE FOR YOU TO GET RIGHT WITH GOD. IF SO, ASK GOD TO REMOVE ANYTHING THAT STANDS BETWEEN YOU AND HIM.

Question: *How can I be sure that I'm saved, even if I don't feel like I'm saved?*

Answer: *I sure feel happy sometimes. And I sure feel sad at other times. And then there are times that I'm sure that I'm not sure how I feel.*

I'm focusing on two key words in your question: "sure" and "feel." When you add salvation to the mix, you're apt to get mixed up.

What I mean is this: you can feel sure that you are saved and yet not be saved. And the opposite is also true: you can be saved and sure not feel like it. (Yes, it's even possible to feel lost and be lost, just as it's possible to feel saved and actually be saved.)

Your question has more to do with times of doubt. This often happens when you've done something that you don't think a follower of Jesus should do (like gossip about somebody behind their back and really enjoy it!), or when you don't do something that you think a follower of Jesus would do (like neglecting to spend time in private devotions).

If you're doing something wrong, then stop! Change! When you stop and change what you're doing wrong, there's a term for it: repent. It means that you don't want things to continue that way, and you even want to undo the bad things that have already happened. That's good! So repent.

This could mean that you go to the people you enjoyed gossiping with and say something like, "You know when I shared that personal information about Jeremy and Tasha (and gave it my own twist), it seemed like fun to talk about them at the time, but now I'm really sorry I did that. I wish I could take it all back. Will you forgive me for talking about them behind their backs? And feel free to stop me if I do something like that again."

Then you may need to go to Jeremy and Tasha and confess to them what you've done, confess your sorrow for doing it, and request that they forgive you (um, they might not be very happy when they find out you were gossiping about them, but they might have already heard from someone else that you did).

And you should definitely come clean with God. You've blown it. Own up to it. Confess it. Release it. Embrace God's forgiveness for you. And if you need a refresher course on this, check out Psalm 51—David's prayer of confession to God after he blew it big-time!

If you doubt your salvation, it might be a nudge for you to get right with God. If so, ask God to remove anything that stands between you and Him.

If you're straight with God, and you're still doubting your salvation, here's what I suggest—it's what I do. Turn to 1 John 5:11-13. Here's how it reads in the *New International Version* (with my comments in parenthesis):

"And this is the testimony: God has given us eternal life, and this life is in his Son." (Instead of accepting your feelings about whether or not you really are saved, go with the testimony that God has given, which is: God has already given you eternal life, so it's already a done deal! Your eternal life is based on God's gift of Jesus, not on whether or not you happen to be feeling it at the moment.)

"He who has the Son has life; he who does not have the Son of God does not have life." (You can't get more simple than this: If you have Jesus, then you have eternal life. If you don't have Jesus, then you don't have eternal life. Now the question changes from Do I have eternal life? to Do I have Jesus? If you have Jesus, you have eternal life. If you aren't sure, then invite Him into your life right now! That's it!)

"I write these things to you who believe in the name of the Son of God so that you may know that you have eternal life." (That's for people like you and me who don't fully believe the previous paragraph. John wrote this so that we can *know* that we have eternal life. Notice that John didn't use the word "feel"—he used the word "know.")

If you want another run at it, check out some previous verses—1 John 3:18-24.

It's wonderful to feel saved. It's even better to be saved. When you have Jesus, it's *the best*!

"He who has the Son has life; he who does not have the Son of God does not have life."

What About Growing Up with Jesus but not Loving Him?

TO "BELONG TO CHRIST JESUS" MEANS TRUSTING HIM INSTEAD OF OUR NATURAL SINFULNESS.

Question: *I've grown up in an Adventist home, but I don't really love Jesus, even though I want to go to heaven. And when I do something wrong, I'm not usually sorry I did it. What can I do?*

Answer: *Growing up in an Adventist home has some major advantages. But it doesn't "guarantee" your personal choices or circumstances.*

Y*ou also mentioned that your motivation for wanting to love Jesus is selfish—so you can go to heaven. I realize that most of our motivations can be traced to selfishness. I agree that a desire to go to heaven can be selfish. Did you realize,* *though, that heaven is all about Jesus? And if you aren't into Jesus, going to heaven will be more like hell than heaven. And Jesus wouldn't put you through that kind of eternal torment.*

Your current experience might be the double life Paul describes in Romans 7: "I don't understand myself at all, for I really want to do what is right, but I don't do it. Instead, I do the very thing I hate" (verse 15, NLT).

"When I want to do good, I don't. And when I try not to do wrong, I do it anyway" (verse 19, NLT).

"Oh, what a miserable person I am! Who will free me from this life that is dominated by sin?" (verse 24, NLT).

"In my mind I really want to obey God's law, but because of my sinful nature I am a slave to sin" (verse 25, NLT).

So what's a person to do? Paul provides the answer as his letter spills into Romans 8: "There is no condemnation for those who belong to Christ Jesus" (verse 1, NLT).

To "belong to Christ Jesus" means trusting Him instead of our natural sinfulness. Read all of Romans 8 to build up your hope. It ends with the promise that nothing is able to separate us from God's love. Maybe you need to start thinking about God's love for you, rather than your love for God. The reason you don't feel badly about doing what's wrong is because you're not feeling love for Jesus.

Jesus told a story that might also relate to you. Two people owed money to the same person: one owed 500 pieces of silver, and the other owed 50. Neither could repay their debt, so the creditor forgave them both. Now, who will love the creditor more?

Of course, the one who's been forgiven more. Jesus said, "Your heart will be where your treasure is" (Matthew 6:21, NCV). So start investing, putting your treasure in Jesus, and your love for Him will grow. Your treasure is your time, your money, your friendships, and your out-of-school activities. Here are two ideas for investing in Jesus:

1. Dust off your Bible and start praying through the stories about Jesus in Matthew, Mark, Luke, and John. Pray or meditate on what it would've been like to be in the places of different people in the story.

2. Do something for somebody else, especially those who can't pay you back or who don't even know you did it. Try doing at least one thing each week.

If you start making these two investments, and after a month you don't find any change in your love for Jesus, write to me again. Tell me about your investments, and let me know where your heart is headed.

"Your heart will be where your treasure is." (Matthew 6:21, NCV)

What About Getting Saved By the Time Jesus Returns?

Question: *How can I stop worrying about whether or not I'm "good enough" to be saved? And what's going to happen before the Second Coming? Will my loved ones be saved?*

Answer: *I count three questions here and they seem to be on the topic of you and your loved ones being saved by the time Jesus returns. I'd like to answer them one at a time.*

Your first question, the one where you refer to worrying about whether or not you're "good enough" to be saved, is an easy one to answer. Stop worrying! There's no need to worry or question this one at all. You're NOT good enough to be saved,

88

and you never will be! The apostle Paul quotes from Psalm 14:1-3 and Psalm 53:1-3 when he writes, "No one is good—not even one. No one has real understanding; no one is seeking God. All have turned away from God; all have gone wrong. No one does good, not even one" (Romans 3:10-12, NLT).

But that doesn't mean you're without hope. Just place your hope somewhere other than "being good enough" yourself. Paul continues later in the chapter, "We are made right in God's sight when we trust in Jesus Christ to take away our sins. And we all can be saved in this same way, no matter who we are or what we have done" (Romans 3:22, NLT).

Some people think that Jesus will forgive us of all of our sins at one point, but from then on we have to be good enough ourselves. But that's not how it works. Jesus not only forgives us, but he continues to forgive us. That means that our part is to turn to Him, to rely on Him, to cling to Him, not only when we first ask for the gift of forgiveness, but every step of the way after that, too.

Don't worry about whether you're good enough to be saved, because you aren't! Jesus offered to trade places with you, so accept that offer, and cling to it! Here's how Paul put it in 2 Corinthians 8:9 (NLT), "You know how full of love and kindness our Lord Jesus Christ was. Though he was very rich, yet for your sakes he became poor, so that by his poverty he could make you rich."

In your second question you asked, "What's going to happen before the Second Coming (of Jesus)?" I must admit that I'm not sure where you're going with that question. Are you asking for signs that Christ's return is near? Are you wondering how much time you and your loved ones have to get it together with God before it all comes to an end?

If you're looking for signs of Christ's return, most people like to go through various lists or phrases they find in Matthew 24. But some people misread these. For example, "wars and rumors of wars" sometimes gets repeated as a sign that Jesus will arrive shortly. But here's how Matthew 24:6 (TLB) actually reads, "When you hear of wars beginning, this does not signal my return; these must come, but the end is not yet." Wars are not the end. They have been going on throughout the history of this world.

Contrast that with Matthew 24:14 (TLB), "And the Good News about the Kingdom will be preached throughout the whole world, so that all nations will hear it, and then, finally, the end will come." Once everyone has the Good News, it's over.

Here's another text often referred to when people talk about the end of the world, "When the Son of Man returns, it will be like it was in Noah's day. In those days before the Flood, the people were enjoying banquets and parties and weddings right up to the time Noah entered his boat. People didn't realize what was going to happen until the Flood came and swept them all away. That is the way it will be when the Son of Man comes" (Matthew 24:37-39, NLT).

Does this means that when the earth is as wicked as it was in the days of Noah, God will once again bring history to an end? Or does it mean that some things will continue, like banquets and parties, right up to the end and people will be surprised that the end was right in front of them? Maybe it means both.

One thing is certain—trying to gauge the time Jesus returns so you can get in at the last minute isn't the way to go. If you think it's like playing basketball by the lakeside while people load a boat and you can leave the game and run and make a jump for the boat as it pulls away, you're going to be left behind! According to Matthew 24:44 (NLT), "You also must be ready all the time. For the Son of Man will come when least expected." If you're waiting until the last moment, you probably won't even see the boat depart!

Waiting until the last minute is not only being foolish and risky; it's missing the point. Let me explain it like this: If you're engaged and will be married in one week, are you going to spend that week going out with as many people of the opposite sex as possible? What kind of commitment would that be? "Hey sweetheart, because I love you so much, I want to go out with everyone I can, except you. I'm afraid that once I'm married to you, I will be trapped. Because I want to be faithful to you, I'm going out with everyone while I'm engaged to you, but at least I'm not married to you." You've got to wonder what kind of marriage that is going to be.

This leads into your third question, "Will my loved ones be saved?" The simple answer is, "I don't know." Do they have Jesus? If they do, they are saved; if they don't, they aren't saved (see 1 John 5:11-13).

Maybe a better question is, "What can you do about your loved ones and their salvation?" My answer to that question is to get together with Jesus yourself. You can't force others, but you can choose for yourself.

Notice the flow that Paul described, and this pertains to you, "When anyone is joined to Christ, he is a new being; the old is gone, the new has come. All this is done by God, who through Christ changed us from enemies into his friends and gave us the task of making others his friends also. . . Here we are, then, speaking for Christ, as though God himself were making his appeal through us. We plead on Christ's behalf: let God change you from enemies into his friends!" (2 Corinthians 5:17-18, 21, TEV).

For God, putting off a decision with Him is always a bad move. His message is never for "tomorrow" but always for "now" or for "today" (see 2 Corinthians 6:2). That's true for you as well as for your loved ones.

When it comes to drawing your loved ones to Jesus, don't forget the two powerful metaphors Jesus gave in the Sermon on the Mount: salt and light. "You are the salt of the earth" (Matthew 5:13) and "You are the light of the world" (Matthew 5:14). As salt, go to where your loved ones are and mix with them so that your influence impacts them. As light, be the person God wants you to be and it will expose bad for what it is and will draw attention to God, not to you (see Matthew 5:16).

I would summarize my answers to all three questions as "Get with God yourself and live for Him forever, starting right now." And I'll see you and your loved ones in heaven!

What About Creation and Evolution?

THE BIBLE BEGINS WITH THE "FACT" THAT GOD CREATED NOT ONLY THIS EARTH, BUT ALSO THE HEAVENS.

(GENESIS 1:1)

Question: *I believe that God created the world, but in public school we're taught about evolution. The teachers say it's a fact. Who's right? How can I tell?*

Answer: *Creation or evolution—which one is right?*

You say that you believe God created the world. Why do you believe that? Is it something you heard while you were growing up, so it seems obvious or normal to you? Is it because you read it in a book? Were you present when it happened so you can say "I saw it!"?

Let's ask the same questions of your public school teacher and consider if the answers would be any different.

Your public school teacher believes in evolution. Why does s/he believe that? Is it something s/he heard while s/he was growing up, so it seems obvious or normal to him/her? Is it because s/he read it in a book? Was s/he present when it happened so s/he can say "I saw it!"?

I think the answers for both you and your teacher probably are: yes, yes, and no.

Here's a question that those who believe in creation like to throw into the discussion—which came first: a chicken or an egg? We know that chickens lay eggs and we know that eggs become chickens, but which one came first?

I'm a creationist, so I say the chicken came first since God created the birds on the fifth day of creation. Later, the chicken laid some eggs and "produced after it's kind" (see Genesis 1:22). Then a chicken came from the egg and later it laid an egg and so on. . . .

I'm not sure how an evolutionist would answer the same question. Did the chicken eventually come from some other egg that maybe mutated into a chicken? Or did the chicken evolve from some other bird or fish or slime or animal and then it happened to lay an egg that kept its family line going?

Frankly, there is evidence for evolution, just like there's evidence for creation. Neither one is a "proven fact." To believe either one requires that you take a leap of faith based on some evidence, but not enough evidence to "prove" it. Those who think otherwise simply aren't very aware or open to conflicting evidence.

When Charles Darwin's *Origin of the Species* first appeared in 1859, a new option was added for explaining how things started on earth. A few things that have made this option attractive are a "scientific" description plus an explanation that keeps God out of the picture.

I put the word "scientific" in quotation marks because it violates several key rules of science. By taking some small changes that have been observed over time (micro-evolution), some people decided that bigger changes could take place over a longer period of time. This means that if you can't explain something, just project it back another 10-20 million years and you can come up with practically any explanation. Currently, "scientists" have to go back in time about five billion years to provide enough time for all the things they can't explain. Since science is only a few thousand years old, and since the age of "enlightenment" is only a few hundred years old, projecting five billion years ago is ludicrous in my opinion.

Perhaps you've heard the story of a young tour guide who took a group of tourists to see some cave paintings. He informed the visitors that the paintings were 10,000,002 years old. Someone asked how he knew it to the exact year. He explained, "Some expert came here and told us that they were 10 million years old. That was two years ago."

You may have heard of scientific discoveries and explanations that later got revised. True scientists limit themselves to what they are able to observe, document, and replicate.

Even though there are incredible creations that take place all the time with plants, animals, and the birth of a baby, we haven't had another creation of the world like the original, and we don't expect one until Jesus brings this earth to a close and creates a "new earth" (see Revelation 21:1).

While science always seeks to "prove" things, there are changes and new discoveries that make previous "facts" no longer facts. For example, the first president of the United States, George Washington, died because the best scientists of the day knew that disease was carried by the blood, so sick people were bled on purpose to get the bad blood out. That was the scientific way to deal with disease at that time. Washington went through three bleedings in a row, which got rid of about a third of the blood in his body. That's when he died (see www.doctorzebra.com/prez/g01.htm). Did the scientific "facts" in Washington's day help him?

Science is limited to what it can observe or make happen. For example, scientists can observe a hurricane, but they can't say exactly where it will go or what damage will result. Scientists can create a mini-hurricane on a computer or in a fish tank, but that's not the same as the real thing. On a daily basis, there are weather reports that are based on "scientific facts" that tell us how hot or cold it will be, as well as how much rain or snow there will be. How often do these "scientific facts" actually turn out the way scientists tell us?

Science differs from superstition (which has been a good arena for the supernatural and expectations from God). Superstition or myth might explain a hurricane as the anger of the sea or water gods. A simple rain shower might be regarded as the tears of a god. Many cultures have named the sun a god and worshiped it because they recognized how dependent they were on it. Here's what Paul had to say about such superstition:

"From the time the world was created, people have seen the earth and sky and all that God made. They can clearly see his invisible qualities—his eternal power and divine nature. So they have no excuse whatsoever for not knowing God. Yes, they knew God, but they wouldn't worship him as God or even give him thanks. . . Claiming to be wise, they became utter fools instead" (Romans 1:20-22, NLT).

There are plenty of stories from Greek, Chinese, Indian, African, or Scandinavian myths about a supernatural start to our earth. Those who prefer a scientific explanation would put the Biblical story of creation in the same category as a myth (see www.magictails.com/creationlinks.html for more examples of creation myths).

Here's something I happened to read recently during my personal devotions. It's a few verses from Isaiah 40. The context is that God's people, who had been following idols, are being asked if they want to follow idols or God. "To whom should we compare our God? What god can we compare Him to? He's not like an idol that a craftsman makes from metal, which the goldsmith overlays with gold and sets on a base made of silver. Do you people not know? Have you not heard? Weren't you told long before this? Haven't you heard how the world began? Look up to the heavens. Who created the universe and all the stars you see? Who guides them through space and calls them all by name? His power and mighty strength are so great, not one of them gets lost" (Isaiah 40:18, 19, 21, 26, *The Clear Word*).

The Bible begins with the "fact" that God created not only this earth, but also the heavens (Genesis 1:1). But for scientists who weren't present, that isn't apt to convince them. As they piece together evidence these days, some conclude that God created it all. Others conclude that natural selection (evolution) is a better explanation. And some have come up with a combination (the "Big Bang" or the option of creation over thousands of years instead of one week).

True scientists will share what they know and will keep looking for more, even when it changes what they understood earlier. Isn't that what everyone has to do as they "grow up"? So, keep growing!

For those who think Darwin's natural selection is the only believable option, try reading *Darwin's Black Box* by Michael Behe. This biochemist points out that simplifying creation to natural selection doesn't work on a biochemical level. That's pretty significant on a scientific level! If you'd like a more comprehensive explanation from scientists who believe in creation, check out *The Case for the Creator* by Lee Strobel.

Creationists are calling these explanations "Intelligent Design" to point out that the evidence from science today points out that something is behind the incredible creation of earth. "Intelligent Design" doesn't necessarily have to be "God," but everyone knows that's what is meant. I don't expect schools (or courts) to approve this being taught when they want to keep God out of the textbooks.

By the way, if you believe in evolution (natural selection), you have no purpose in life except to survive and beat out others who are going for the same things you are. Don't share or give anything to others unless you're certain to get paid back so you can get ahead. Exploit others because everyone is on his own; it's survival of the fittest, baby! And our society shouldn't waste our precious resources on the weak. Wipe out all who are handicapped, retarded, or "challenged." They are a waste. (I'm not suggesting that you do this; I'm simply pointing out that this would be consistent with natural selection.) Do you want to live in an environment like that?

If you believe in creation, you are a child of God. God has given you talents to develop so you can create for the benefit of others, which glorifies God. The more you give away, the more God gives to you! Give special attention to those who are weak—what you do for them is what you are actually doing to God. (I am suggesting, actually I'm urging that you do this; it's consistent with creation and redemption.) Do you want to live in an environment like this?

While you and I (and all scientists) were not present at creation, the same Creator is still creating things today. According to 2 Corinthians 5:17, when an individual gives his/her life to God, that person becomes a new "creation." If there's no evidence of the creator still actively creating in our world right now, who cares about whether or not He was there at the start! Can you find a Creator at work today in your life and around your world?

According to 2 Corinthians 5:17, when an individual gives his/her life to God, that person becomes a new "creation."

What About When Prayer Doesn't Work?

"In my distress I prayed to the Lord, and the Lord answered me and rescued me. The Lord is for me, so I will not be afraid. What can mere mortals do to me?"

(Psalm 118:5, 6)

Question: *God's not hearing me. I pray, but nothing happens. He's answering my friends' prayers, though. Why?*

Answer: *Actually, God is listening and answering your prayers and your friends' prayers. But we usually think of God listening or answering only when we seem to be getting the results we want.*

Perhaps what you need to do is change what you're saying in your prayers. For example, instead of asking God for merely good grades, ask Him to teach you what you need to know. Rather than asking God for a special someone to like you, ask God to help you care about somebody you can't stand right now.

I can't explain why so many things happen the way they do. But I can tell you that I've found that the Psalms are a great resource for me when it seems like God is listening, and when it seems like He isn't doing anything about my situation.

I've underlined certain parts in the Psalms so I can find them quickly, whether I want to shout to God for joy or to cry out to Him in anger or frustration. The Psalms can become your prayers too. Check out these passages from the *New Living Translation*. Circle the ones you'll want to pray when it seems like God is listening. Underline the ones you'll want to pray when it seems like He isn't listening.

"Unless the Lord had helped me, I would soon have died. I cried out, 'I'm slipping!' and your unfailing love, O Lord, supported me. When doubts filled my mind, your comfort gave me renewed hope and cheer" (Psalm 94:17-19).

"I cry out to God without holding back. Oh, that God would listen to me!" (Psalm 77:1).

"Praise God, who did not ignore my prayer and did not withdraw his unfailing love from me" (Psalm 66:20).

"In my distress I prayed to the Lord, and the Lord answered me and rescued me. The Lord is for me, so I will not be afraid. What can mere mortals do to me?" (Psalm 118:5, 6).

"Has the Lord rejected me forever? Will he never again show me favor? Is his unfailing love gone forever? Have his promises permanently failed? Has God forgotten to be kind? Has he slammed the door on his compassion?" (Psalm 77:7-9).

"Guide my steps by your word, so I will not be overcome by any evil" (Psalm 119:133).

"Give us gladness in proportion to our former misery! Replace the evil years with good. Let us see your miracles again; let our children see your glory at work" (Psalm 90:15, 16).

"The Lord says, 'I will guide you along the best pathway for your life. I will advise you and watch over you'" (Psalm 32:8).

"Commit everything you do to the Lord. Trust him, and he will help you" (Psalm 37:5).

"Why am I discouraged? Why so sad? I will put my hope in God! I will praise him again—my Savior and my God!" (Psalm 43:5).

I can't give you a quick-fix answer as to why it seems that God answers some prayers but ignores others. However, I have found it helpful to use the Psalms as my prayers rather than getting bitter and cutting myself off from God.

It sounds like you're very close to actually praying by wrestling with God. That's a completely different world compared to reciting a wish list to Him. Welcome to deeper levels of intimacy with God! Welcome to an experience of listening to God instead of merely talking to Him.

"Commit everything you do to the Lord. Trust him, and he will help you." (Psalm 37:5)

What About Feeling Close to God?

INSTEAD OF BEING

FRUSTRATED

ABOUT THE

THINGS YOU

DON'T

UNDERSTAND IN

THE BIBLE, FOCUS

ON THE THINGS

YOU DO

UNDERSTAND.

Question: *Even though I know God and He's real in my life, how can I get a one-on-one, really close, personal relationship with Him? I have friends who seem to have it, and I envy them sometimes. But no matter how hard I pray and study my Bible (and I don't understand half of what I read), that kind of relationship doesn't happen for me. Do you think the devil has anything to do with this?*

Answer: *I'm pleased and excited to hear you say that you have a relationship with Jesus already. But I wonder if that means you've simply accepted Jesus, but haven't done much to develop your relationship with Him.*

101

Y*ou mentioned that you read your Bible and pray, but that it doesn't do much for your relationship with God— well, so far it hasn't produced the kind of relationship that your friends seem to have with Jesus. I suggest that you ask your friends what they do to make their one-on-one relationship with Jesus thrive.*

Here's what I do. Yes, I read the Bible, and I pray. But that isn't enough. Those devotional disciplines come to life when I start living what I've read and prayed. In fact, my prayers often get shaped by what I've read in the Bible.

I'm quite a bit older than you, and I still don't understand everything in the Bible. But I read for the purpose of making contact with God. I've found that when I read "because I'm supposed to," it's more like a classroom assignment than a relationship. For example, if a teacher told me I had to become close friends with another person, that wouldn't motivate me as much as if I wanted to become friends with him or her.

Instead of being frustrated about the things you don't understand in the Bible, focus on the things you do understand. Try reading Matthew 5, 6, and 7. It won't take long to read those chapters. Afterward, take time to pray about one verse a day. Then look for ways that God can live that verse through you. Here are a few examples:

Go out of your way to do incredible things for people you don't like, and people who don't like you for some reason. (see Matthew 5:44)

Give things to people who need them without making a show of it or doing it for community service credit. (see Matthew 6:2) If you aren't giving anything to the needy, then start.

Ask God to forgive you only as often as you forgive people who do you wrong. (That's in the middle of the Lord's Prayer in Matthew 6:12.) What would happen to you if God forgave you only when you forgave others?

In everything you do, treat others the way you would want them to treat you. (Check out the "Golden Rule" in Matthew 7:12.)

My guess is that if you zero in on parts of the Bible such as those, you'll start to pray more, because you'll be desperate for God to change you on the inside. And that's when you'll find your one-on-one relationship with God becoming more than just a nice thing. It'll be the focus of your entire life.

Do you really want a one-on-one relationship with Jesus? How about having that kind of relationship with both Jesus and God the Father? In Jesus' words: "All those who love me will do what I say. My Father will love them, and we will come to them and live with them" (John 14:23, NLT).

In everything you do, treat others the way you would want them to treat you.

What About Spiritual Warfare?

IF YOU RELY ON YOUR OWN STRENGTH TO RESIST TEMPTATION, YOU'LL LOSE EVERY TIME. BECAUSE WE HAVE A SINFUL NATURE THAT FEELS RIGHT AT HOME WITH TEMPTATION, I STILL THINK IT'S A GOOD IDEA TO PHYSICALLY WALK OR EVEN RUN AWAY FROM TEMPTATIONS—AS JOSEPH RAN AWAY FROM POTIPHAR'S WIFE.

Question: *I've been struggling with a particular sin. I want to know why I feel so weak to temptation, even when I call to Jesus in prayer. Is it because I'm relying on my own strength to resist? Or is it because it's a spiritual battle, and I have to fight it with spiritual things?*

Answer: *Sin, temptation, and prayer are definitely ingredients for a spiritual battle. And you've already been utilizing the great spiritual weapon of prayer.*

Before we look at a text about spiritual warfare, let's first consider a text about temptation. Notice the progression in this sequence: "God is never tempted to *do wrong, and he never tempts anyone else either. Temptation comes from the lure of our own evil desires. These evil desires lead to evil actions, and evil actions lead to death" (James 1:13-16, NLT).*

If you rely on your own strength to resist temptation, you'll lose every time. Because we have a sinful nature that feels right at home with temptation, I still think it's a good idea to physically walk or even run away from temptations—as Joseph ran away from Potiphar's wife (Genesis 39:12).

Paul wrote, "When you follow the desires of your sinful nature, your lives will produce these evil results: sexual immorality, . . . idolatry, participation in demonic activities, hostility, quarreling, jealousy, outbursts of anger, selfish ambition, divisions, the feeling that everyone is wrong except those in your own little group, envy, drunkenness, wild parties, and other kinds of sin. Let me tell you again, as I have before, that anyone living that sort of life will not inherit the Kingdom of God" (Galatians 5:19-21, NLT).

When you continue reading this passage, there's some good news: "But when the Holy Spirit controls our lives, he will produce this kind of fruit in us: love, joy, peace, patience, kindness, goodness, faithfulness, gentleness, and self-control. Here there is no conflict with the law. Those who belong to Christ Jesus have nailed the passions and desires of their sinful nature to his cross and crucified them there" (verses 22-25, NLT).

When I face temptation, I need God's power to overcome it. But I also need God to change my desires, since I naturally want what the temptation offers me. So my prayer is for power from God to overcome temptation and to change me.

My youth pastor friend Brett Hadley shares with young people that sin is SAD—Seductive, Addictive, Destructive. Sin seduces us by luring us into what it offers. Next it becomes addictive—instead of sin chasing you, you begin to chase it. And finally sin destroys you. If not now, it will destroy you for eternity.

You mentioned that you've been praying. Right on! Check out Ephesians 6:10-18 for more spiritual weapons to use in battle, such as truth, God's righteousness, peace, the gospel, faith, salvation, Scripture, and persistent praying. Why not utilize all the weapons God has provided for you?

When I face temptation, I need God's power to overcome it. But I also need God to change my desires, since I naturally want what the temptation offers me. So my prayer is for power from God to overcome temptation and to change me.

What About Getting Baptized?

DOES BAPTISM

SAVE TEENS—OR

ANYBODY ELSE?

OF COURSE NOT.

ONLY JESUS DOES.

(SEE ACTS 4:12)

Question: *I'm 15 years old, and I'm not baptized. Everyone seems to be jumping all over me about it—someone even said I was awful. Now I'm building up a grudge against being baptized. Do you blame me? What should I do?*

Answer: *When I was 15 years old, I didn't appreciate anyone telling me what to do—about anything. And when they acted as if they were the voice of God for me, it made me even more reluctant to respond. So I identify with what you're going through.*

Take a wild trip with me through your imagination. Let's pretend that you're an adult, and you see a teenager at your *church. You realize that even though young people grow up going to church, that doesn't mean they've chosen Jesus for themselves.*

You want that teen to be in heaven. And you know that the only way they'll be in heaven is if they choose Jesus for themselves. So you assume, If the teen is baptized and accepts Jesus, that teen will be in heaven.

Once that's settled, you quit worrying about that teen. But you might bug them if you see them doing something you don't think young people headed for heaven should be doing.

Now, here's a question about your assumption: Does baptism save teens—or anybody else? Of course not. Only Jesus does (see Acts 4:12). However, baptism does signify that a person, regardless of their age, has chosen to end their life of selfishness and start a new one centered around Jesus.

Paul said it this way: "Have you forgotten that when we became Christians and were baptized to become one with Christ Jesus, we died with him? For we died and were buried with Christ by baptism. And just as Christ was raised from the dead by the glorious power of the Father, now we also may live new lives" (Romans 6:3, 4, NLT).

Now back to your situation. I'm curious to know why you haven't been baptized. I'm not trying to force you to be baptized. I'm just wondering if you've chosen Jesus to be the center of your life.

If you haven't, don't just go through the motions to please somebody else. It has to be your choice. If you aren't friends with Jesus, it doesn't make sense to get baptized.

But if you're already friends with Jesus, then I need to ask you if you're ready to commit your life to Him. If you are, then go for baptism. If you aren't, then continue to grow in your relationship with Him.

Baptism, like a wedding, is a symbol that means a lot. Some people may say that a baptism or a wedding is no big deal. But most people would disagree. Sure, you can just go through the motions, but why play around with commitments that are so special?

At 15 you're old enough to make some major decisions, especially when it comes to choosing Jesus to be the center of your life. Making that decision will actually help you make all your other decisions too! But whether or not you decide to follow Jesus is up to you—no matter what anyone says.

> "Have you forgotten that when we became Christians and were baptized to become one with Christ Jesus, we died with him? For we died and were buried with Christ by baptism. And just as Christ was raised from the dead by the glorious power of the Father, now we also may live new lives."
>
> (Romans 6:3, 4, NLT)

What About Spiritual Growth?

"THE LORD HAS ALREADY TOLD YOU WHAT IS GOOD, AND THIS IS WHAT HE REQUIRES: TO DO WHAT IS RIGHT, TO LOVE MERCY, AND TO WALK HUMBLY WITH YOUR GOD."

(MICAH 6:8, NLT)

Question: *What would help me reach the spiritual height that God wants for me?*

Answer: *My mind races to several well-known Scriptures, such as Isaiah 58:13, 14. This passage talks about making the Sabbath a delight instead of just doing your own thing. "Then you will find your joy in the Lord, and I will cause you to ride on the heights of the land and to feast on the inheritance of your father Jacob" (verse 14).*

It seems to me that many people lose out on the spiritual height God desires for them because their focus on Sabbath is on "me, me, me" instead of on "Thee, Thee, Thee."

There's also Jeremiah 29:11. It says, "'I know the plans I have for you,' declares the Lord, 'plans to prosper you and not to harm you, plans to give you hope and a future.'" That promise can motivate people to discover and pursue God's desires for them.

How about this verse? "The Lord has already told you what is good, and this is what he requires: to do what is right, to love mercy, and to walk humbly with your God" (Micah 6:8, NLT). Practicing these things could impact every area of a person's life.

When the religious leaders asked Jesus for the greatest commandment, He replied with two: to love God and to love others as yourself (see Matthew 22:34-40). Compare that with Micah 6:8, and you'll have the guidelines you need for soaring to the heights God has in mind for you.

Now let's talk about Jesus' paradoxes—His statements that seem not to make sense if you look at things the way most people do. Here's a classic example: "The greatest among you must be a servant" (Matthew 23:11, NLT).

Using that statement to answer your question about attaining the spiritual height God desires for you, I'd say you should go "low" in order to get spiritual height. In practical terms, going "low" would mean to do whatever you can to serve others. There's nothing better you can do.

Some would argue that spending time in personal devotions, such as meditating on Scripture, is the most important thing to do. I'd place such solitary activities as number two, not number one.

The most important thing is to serve others. Contact with God can be found in personal meditation and in service to others. If you have only personal meditation and lack service to others, your personal meditation will self-destruct into nothingness.

To attain the heights God desires for you, accept His gift of salvation. Then live for God by serving others.

I like the way Paul stated it in Ephesians 2:8-10 (NLT): "God saved you by his special favor when you believed. And you can't take credit for this; it is a gift from God. Salvation is not a reward for the good things we have done, so none of us can boast about it. For we are God's masterpiece. He has created us anew in Christ Jesus, so that we can do the good things he planned for us long ago."

"The greatest among you must be a servant." (Matthew 23:11, NLT)

What About Revival!

"THIS PEOPLE'S
HEART HAS
BECOME
CALLOUSED; THEY
HARDLY HEAR
WITH THEIR EARS,
AND THEY HAVE
CLOSED THEIR
EYES."

(MATTHEW 13:15)

Question: *We have the truth, but we're not preaching it the way we should. Worse than that, we've become so familiar with the Word of God that we aren't living by what we know to be right. We need spiritual revival, but how can we get it?*

Answer: *Usually when I hear, "We need spiritual renewal and revival," it comes from somebody who's frustrated that more people aren't sincere or enthusiastic about spiritual things. I've felt that way. And sometimes I've heard others say that type of thing when I wasn't spiritually "on fire" myself.*

*H*as the same been true for you—sometimes you're hot, sometimes lukewarm, sometimes cold? Or do you find yourself to be a constant source of inspiration to others, proclaiming a consistent testimony, perpetually serving others, and listening to those who are distraught?

A broad question such as "We need spiritual revival, but how can we get it?" deserves a response. But I'm not sure that you and I have the same experience with Adventists, or even if we've been to the same Adventist churches. I can make some guesses as to why you or others feel as though the church needs spiritual revival:

1. Jesus hasn't returned, and it's hard to wait any longer.

2. Life has become too boring.

3. The church seems to be for old people.

4. Members don't care about "truth"—they just want to have fun.

Try creating a list of your own. Try creating one with your youth group or even some adults.

I think you'll find that Jesus' parable about the sower (we'd call the person a farmer) will provide some answers to your questions. You can find it in Matthew 13:1-23. Verse 15 says, "This people's heart has become calloused; they hardly hear with their ears, and they have closed their eyes."

Verses 18-23 explain the parable. The seed represents the good news about God's kingdom that gets spread all over the place. But sometimes those who hear it are hardened, and the devil snatches the good news away.

Some who hear the good news respond with joy, but they quickly lose their liveliness because it's a shallow experience that hasn't grown any roots. Basically, once tough times come, they quit religion.

Others who hear the good news respond positively. But then the things of this world take precedence, and the good news gets choked out.

The bottom line is that good soil produces a good harvest.

Usually we place guilt on people and tell them to try harder or to get more serious or to put forth more energy toward God. It might last for a short time. But according to the parable, the problem is with the soil.

What is needed is proper soil preparation. If your heart is hard, it needs to be plowed up and turned over and probably broken up quite a bit. If you're living in rocky soil, the rocks need to be removed in order for the good news about the kingdom to take root. Or if you're mixing the things of the world with the good news of the kingdom, then the kingdom will get squeezed out.

If you want a spiritual crop, you need to prepare the soil. Are you ready to lead the way and have your life be turned upside down, sifted, weeded, and some things removed? If not, don't ask others to do it either. But if you are ready, why not lead the way by first being an example? Then, when others see the good that results, they'll be directed to God (see Matthew 5:16).

If you want a spiritual crop, you need to prepare the soil.

Questions About the Bible

- ◆ PREDESTINATION AND FREEDOM OF CHOICE?
- ◆ DEATH?
- ◆ HELL?
- ◆ THE RICH MAN, LAZARUS AND HELL?
- ◆ BEING "LEFT BEHIND"?
- ◆ THE MILLENNIUM?
- ◆ THE 144,000?
- ◆ SEVEN BEING THE "PERFET" NUMBER?
- ◆ HOMOSEXUALITY?
- ◆ ALL OF THE KILLING IN THE BIBLE?
- ◆ GETTING THE ANIMALS INTO NOAH'S ARK?
- ◆ WOMEN WHO DEFY GOD?
- ◆ A SANCTUARY IN HEAVEN?

What About Predestination and Freedom of Choice?

LET'S CONSIDER WHAT FREEDOM OF CHOICE WE HAVE WHEN IT COMES TO GOD AND LIVING ON THIS PLANET.

Question: *There's a verse in the New Testament that says we were "predestined" to be children of God. How does free choice fit into that idea?*

Answer: *I think the verse you're referring to is either Romans 8:29 or Ephesians 1:5. In the New International Version Romans 8:29 reads, "For those God foreknew he also predestined to be conformed to the likeness of his Son, that he might be the firstborn among many brothers."*

Ephesians 1:5 reads, "He predestined us to be adopted as his sons through Jesus Christ, in accordance with his pleasure and will."

You can find the word "predestined" in Romans 8:30 and Ephesians 1:11, too, used in the same context as it is in Romans 8:29 and Romans 1:5.

Because the United States has the reputation that individual rights and opportunities are abundant, lots of people think that they can control or choose more than they actually can. Idealistic young people imagine that by choosing a career, they will have success in that career.

In many places in the world, people don't think about choice as much as North Americans do. For example, if you live in a caste system, the family or caste you were born into determines your socio-economic status for life. If you were born with AIDS or were a crack baby, what choices do you have? Nobody has been asked if they want to be born, where they choose to be born, which gender they choose to be, or even who would be their parents. In some cultures, you don't even choose who you will marry.

You didn't choose for tsunamis, earthquakes, or hurricane-producing floods to take place. You didn't choose to have planes crash into the World Trade Center in New York, or to have your country invaded by outsiders.

You may have chosen to vote, but it seemed like your one vote didn't count for much when millions of others voted, too. You may have chosen to befriend somebody, but that doesn't mean that they chose to become your friend. You may have chosen to go out for a sport and even practiced to make the team, but that doesn't mean that the coach chose you to be on the team.

Let's consider what freedom of choice we have when it comes to God and living on this planet. Look earlier in the book of Romans for some keys to understanding Romans 8:29. We can find that the heathen are "without excuse" for not worshiping God (see Romans 1:18-20). We also find that the followers of God are also "without excuse" for not truly following God (see Romans 2:1, 17-24). This gets summarized in Romans 3:23 (NIV), "For all have sinned and fall short of the glory of God."

Paul goes on to explain God's way of dealing with the sin issue. In Romans 6:23 (NLT) you can read, "For the wages of sin is death, but the free gift of God is eternal life through Christ Jesus our Lord."

I think Paul is saying that you and I have earned death. It's the wage that we deserve—because we were born naturally selfish, and we've made plenty of choices along the way that are either totally selfish or mixed with selfishness. But God provides a free gift. Providing the gift isn't my choice, but accepting the gift is.

Notice how Paul presents the element of choice in Romans 6:16-18 (NLT): "Don't you realize that whatever you choose to obey becomes your master? You can choose sin, which leads to death, or you can choose to obey God and receive his approval. Thank God! Once you were slaves of sin, but now you have obeyed with all your heart the new teaching God has given you. Now you are free from sin, your old master, and you have become slaves to your new master, righteousness."

This means that when God "predestined" you to become Christlike, it wasn't a threat; it was a promise. He not only saves you to come to heaven with Him one day, but He enters you now and transforms you to become like Him, starting now! That's God's plan. Your "choice" is whether or not you want that package. If you choose not to, that's your choice, and choices always have consequences. Since you and I are not God, we don't get to negotiate the deal; we simply choose what the deal will be for us.

I'd recommend that you read all of Romans 8 (1-2 pages in most Bibles—I especially like *The Living Bible* for this chapter). Try reading Romans 8:29-30 in *The Message*. And then pray, thanking God for the provision He has made for you—including the choice you have to be a child of God.

I've found that by choosing to be a child of God, I have far more choices than I'd ever get if I didn't choose to be His child.

What About Death?

SOMETIMES CHRISTIANS MISTAKENLY BELIEVE THAT THEIR GOOD WORKS WILL GET THEM TO HEAVEN INSTEAD OF TRUSTING JESUS TO PROVIDE THEM WITH THIS GIFT THAT THEY CAN'T OBTAIN THEMSELVES.

(SEE EPHESIANS 2:8, 9)

Question: *I told my friend that when a person dies, it's like they're asleep until Jesus returns and resurrects them. But she says that when people die, they go to a kingdom and wait there until the Lord comes. How do I tell her that when people die, they don't really go anywhere?*

Answer: *What happens after a person dies has been a topic of high interest from the beginning of time. In virtually all religions and civilizations there's a common belief that some type of life exists after life on this earth. And the way you get it is by being good while you're on earth, or else by pleasing someone in the other realm who can get you there.*

Sometimes Christians mistakenly believe that their good works will get them to heaven instead of trusting Jesus to provide them with this gift that they can't obtain themselves (see Ephesians 2:8, 9).

Another emphasis is reincarnation—if you're not good enough in this life, you get to do a rerun next time and the next . . . . Not surprisingly, people who believe this way aren't motivated to do much. They'll just try next time rather than right now.

I know one religion that teaches that if you're really good in this life, you'll be given a planet of your own. Perhaps that's a variation of getting a kingdom.

Another popular Christian religion teaches that after you die, you go to one of three places—heaven if you're good; hell if you're bad; or purgatory if you've been a combination of good and bad.

If you're in purgatory, you can get to heaven if you get special favors either from heaven or from those on earth praying for you or giving money to the church on your behalf. Otherwise you'll eventually end up in hell. How's that for a fund-raiser!

Some interesting behaviors are practiced by people who rely on getting a good afterlife by pleasing someone in the other realm. To get their gods' attention they do bizarre things, such as sacrifice their children, walk on burning coals, make pilgrimages through torturous conditions, mutilate their bodies, etc. They do these things hoping it will all be worthwhile in the end.

Christians, by name, are believers in Jesus Christ, which means we trust Jesus to save us from our sins (Matthew 1:21) and to provide us with eternal life (Romans 6:23). Christians look to Jesus as the source of life and the source to help us find out about life. We consult the Bible as a record of the life and teachings of Jesus before, during, and after His time on earth. Let's consider a few passages from the Bible concerning the topic of death and kingdoms. Look up in your Bible what the texts say. I'll just list the texts and provide a few comments.

Genesis 3:3, 4—Eve told Satan that God had said that eating or even touching the fruit from the tree of knowledge of good and evil would result in death. Satan's response was "You won't die." Many people have considered this to be the very first lie recorded in Scripture. And it's a lie that people continue to believe to this day.

Genesis 2:7—A simple equation: dust + God's breath = an alive human being.

Ecclesiastes 12:7—The reverse of the previous equation: an alive human being – God's breath = dust returning to earth. That doesn't sound like another kingdom to me.

John 5:24—Those who hear and believe the message of Jesus have eternal life (starting right now) and have moved from the "kingdom" of death to the "kingdom" of life.

John 3:16—Believers in Jesus have eternal life. All others perish (would you consider that to be a kingdom?).

John 11:11-14—For Jesus, what we consider as "death" is merely like "sleep."

John 11:23-27—The Jews believed in a resurrection at the end of time, not a separate kingdom for dead people. Jesus pointed out that the resurrection is based on Him since He's the source of life.

John 17:3—Eternal life is based on knowing Jesus.

1 John 5:11-13—In case you didn't get it earlier, we're back to a simple equation: you have Jesus = you have eternal life. If you don't have Jesus = you don't have eternal life. There doesn't seem to be any middle ground or other territory or kingdom.

If you'd like a few challenging, isolated verses on this topic, try 1 Peter 3:18-22 or 2 Corinthians 12:2-4. Check them out. Consult with a Bible commentary or ask your pastor or other believers for an explanation. Or feel free to contact me and ask for one.

The idea that many Christians have of people going to heaven right after they die isn't based on the Bible. It has its roots in Greek mythology, which exerted an influence on the early Christian church and continues to do so today.

As far as knowing what happens after you die, perhaps some people will never believe for themselves until it happens to them. But we all know what the resurrection scene will look like. It will include all heaven, earth, and even the devil and his underworld. Get a glimpse of it in Philippians 2:9-11.

As far as knowing what happens after you die, perhaps some people will never believe for themselves until it happens to them.

What About Hell?

WHY DON'T WE—
SEVENTH-DAY
ADVENTISTS—
BELIEVE IN THE
"BIBLICAL TRUTH"
OF HELL? WE DO!

Question: *My parents and I were listening to a Christian radio station in the car the other day, and the speaker was talking about the "biblical truth" of hell. If it's "biblical truth," why don't we believe in it?*

Answer: *Listening to a Christian radio station can be a good thing to do while you're traveling in the car. It sounds like you were listening to a sermon or talk, probably by a local pastor or a better-known pastor that sends sermons and talks on a lot of Christian radio stations.*

If you visit other churches, you'll hear a variety of speakers, just like you'll hear a variety of speakers on Christian radio stations. Most radio preachers are Protestants who believe that Jesus is the way to salvation; the New Testament is for Christians and the Old Testament is for Jews; when Christians die, they go straight to heaven; and when Jesus comes, there will be a secret rapture, as in the "Left Behind" fictional stories.

I don't know about you, but I believe some of the same things as these preachers. I also disagree with some of their beliefs. Do you believe everything that most radio preachers believe? I hope not!

My guess is that you believe what the Bible says, and the radio preacher believes what the Bible says. But how you understand the Bible, and how the radio preacher understands the Bible, might be different.

Shocking news: you shouldn't believe everything a radio preacher says, and the same is true for TV preachers, or the preacher at your own church! You shouldn't believe everything you read in this book, either!

As you get older it's important to investigate issues for yourself, seeking God's guidance before coming to a personal decision on those issues. When a radio preacher or someone else uses a term such as "biblical truth," it leads people who are pro-Bible and pro-truth to swallow whatever comes next. It's sort of like when a person says, "I'm not saying this; God is!" Watch out for people like that. They are susceptible to making God say whatever they want to emphasize.

Okay, back to your question. Why don't we—Seventh-day Adventists—believe in the "biblical truth" of hell? We do!

Just like there are several words for "love" in the Bible (*agape, phileo, eros*), there are several words for "hell" in the Bible. Here they are from the Old Testament (Hebrew) and the New Testament (Greek).

Sheol in the Old Testament and *Hades* in the New Testament are usually translated as "hell" or "grave" or "death," depending on which translation you choose. Examples can be found in places such as Genesis 42:38; Psalm

9:17;1 Kings 2:6; Revelation 1:18. It's what happens when a person dies, whether that person is righteous or wicked (see Genesis 37:35; Numbers 16:30, 33; Matthew 11:23).

The Hebrew location "the Valley of Ben Hinnom" (Joshua 18:16 or Jeremiah 7:31, 32) gets translated as "*Gehenna*" in the New Testament (see Matthew 5:22, 29, 30 or James 3:6). This was the garbage dump outside of Jerusalem, and it was usually burning. It was where you got rid of stuff that you never wanted again. We would call it a fire pit or incinerator nowadays. This was the place where the Israelites sacrificed their children to the heathen god Molech, which met with major disapproval from God (2 Chronicles 28:3-5; 33:6).

There's one more word for "hell" in the Bible: *Tartarus*. It's found only once in the Bible in 2 Peter 2:4. It was thought to be someplace below the grave. It's not surprising that Peter used this term as someplace worse than death, since it was seen as a place where Satan's angels were sent when they were cast out of heaven.

All of us are headed for "hell," meaning "death," until Jesus returns. When Jesus returns, He will resurrect the righteous (1 Thessalonians 4:16, 17). And those who haven't received the gift of eternal life will "perish" in "hell" or "*Gehenna*," "the lake of fire," at the end of the world—a thousand years after Jesus comes to earth and takes the righteous to heaven (John 3:16; Revelation 20:13-15).

That's the truth. Check it out.

All of us are headed for "hell," meaning "death," until Jesus returns. When Jesus returns, He will resurrect the righteous.

What About the Rich Man, Lazarus, and Hell?

THE DECISIONS YOU MAKE NOW AFFECTS YOUR ETERNAL DESTINY.

Question: *Does hell exist? The parable of the rich man and Lazarus shows that it does.*

Answer: *Yes, hell exists, but I'm not sure what you mean by "hell," or what you think the parable of the rich man and Lazarus teaches about hell.*

The parable about the rich man and Lazarus is found only in Luke 16:19-31. Here's how it reads from the New Living Translation: "Jesus said, 'There was a certain rich man who was splendidly clothed and who lived each day in luxury. At his door lay a diseased beggar named Lazarus. As Lazarus lay there longing for scraps from the rich man's table, the dogs *would come and lick his open sores. Finally, the beggar died and was carried by the angels to be with Abraham [in Greek it means Abraham's bosom]. The rich man also died and was buried, and his soul went to the place of the dead [in Greek it means hades]. There, in torment, he saw Lazarus in the far distance with Abraham.*

"The rich man shouted, 'Father Abraham, have some pity! Send Lazarus over here to dip the tip of his finger in water and cool my tongue, because I am in anguish in these flames.'

"But Abraham said to him, 'Son, remember that during your lifetime you had everything you wanted, and Lazarus had nothing. So now he is here being comforted, and you are in anguish. And besides, there is a great chasm separating us. Anyone who wanted to cross over to you from here is stopped at its edge, and no one there can cross over to us.'

"Then the rich man said, 'Please, Father Abraham, send him to my father's home. For I have five brothers, and I want him to warn them about this place of torment so they won't have to come here when they die.'

"But Abraham said, 'Moses and the prophets have warned them. Your brothers can read their writings anytime they want to.'

"The rich man replied, 'No, Father Abraham! But if someone is sent to them from the dead, then they will turn from their sins.'

"But Abraham said, 'If they won't listen to Moses and the prophets, they won't listen even if someone rises from the dead.'"

It's a great story. Because of the Greek influence at that time in history, many people believed that when a person died, they had an immortal (undying) soul that would go on living. This error—based on Greek thought, not the Old Testament—is not the point of the story. The point is, the decisions you make now affects your eternal destiny.

Usually parables have a main point, or a few main points. But not everything in the parable can be carried over into real life, because it just doesn't make much sense if you try to make the parable a literal story. Take for example "Abraham's bosom" (Luke 16:22)—it isn't big enough to fit a man into it or any other poor people who go to heaven. And come on, heaven isn't Abraham's bosom!

In this parable the eternal life of the wicked isn't pleasurable, but it seems to continue. Actually, it sounds like both the righteous and the wicked have eternal life, which isn't consistent with what the Bible says in John 3:16. When a person dies, they go to the grave, which is translated sheol in Hebrew and hades in Greek. And that's the word that's used in Luke 16:23, not the Greek word *gehenna*, which means fire pit.

To me, the most amazing part of the story is the rich man in torment asking for something miraculous—sending Lazarus back from the dead to warn people who are alive. Just a few weeks after Jesus told this story, Jesus resurrected a guy named Lazarus in front of the Pharisees and many other people (see John 11). Even after that the Pharisees didn't turn from their sins and listen to Lazarus or to Jesus. Instead, they decided to kill them both (see John 11:53; 12:9-11).

Yes, hell exists, but not the way it's presented in the parable of the rich man and Lazarus. Just don't make the same mistake the rich man made by thinking a good life now means a good eternity. Get a grip on what God has already revealed in Scripture. Through His Word He desires to guide you and to give purpose to your life.

Get a grip on what God has already revealed in Scripture. Through His Word He desires to guide you and to give purpose to your life.

What About Being "Left Behind"?

BEFORE JESUS LEFT EARTH TO GO TO HEAVEN HE TOLD HIS DISCIPLES THAT HE WAS GOING TO HIS FATHER'S HOUSE TO PREPARE A PLACE FOR THEM.

(JOHN 14:1-3)

Question: *Who's going to be left behind when Jesus comes?*

Answer: *The wording of your question makes me wonder if you've seen the Left Behind movie or read the Left Behind book series. Both the movie and books were quite popular a few years ago, and they've shaped the way a lot of people think about what will happen when Jesus returns.*

The basic idea in the movie and books is that Jesus will come back to earth and secretly "rapture" those who are true to Him. If you don't make it to heaven that time, you'll have seven years of "tribulation." Then, if you were true to Jesus, you can catch Him the next time He

131

returns, which won't be a secret. There's also an emphasis on Jewish people accepting Christ as the Messiah during this tribulation or time of trouble.

I believe Jesus will return, but not the way just described. I don't believe there's a secret coming of Christ, or that He'll come again seven years later.

Here's the passage that mentions "left behind." It's Matthew 24:40, 41: "Two men will be working together in the field; one will be taken, the other left. Two women will be grinding flour at the mill; one will be taken, the other left" (NLT).

By planting the idea that some people will be "left behind" when Jesus comes, there are Christians who interpret those verses as proof that one person will be "taken" to heaven, and the other one will be "left" for seven years of tribulation.

But if you read the three verses before verses 40 and 41, you end up with the opposite meaning. Notice who's "taken": "As it was in the days of Noah, so it will be at the coming of the Son of Man. For in the days before the flood, people were eating and drinking, marrying and giving in marriage, up to the day Noah entered the ark; and they knew nothing about what would happen until the flood came and took them all away. That is how it will be at the coming of the Son of Man" (Matthew 24:37-39).

Did you notice who got "taken"? The ones who were "taken" were the ones outside the ark. In other words, the ones "taken" didn't make it; they died. The ones "left behind" are the ones in the ark, which is where I'd rather be. How about you? See how opposite that is of what a lot of people have been led to believe?

Your question also brings up the basic question about who will go to heaven, and who won't. Answers usually have something to do with salvation instead of sin, of grace rather than works, and of Jesus and not ourselves. If you'd like to look up a few verses on these themes, check out Acts 4:12; Romans 6:23; 1 John 5:11-13; and Ephesians 2:8-10.

Before Jesus left earth to go to heaven He told His disciples that He was going to His Father's house to prepare a place for them (John14:1-3). Later in the same conversation Jesus told the disciples that those who love Him will be the ones who obey Him. And both He and the Father will make their home with them (see John 14:23).

So if you're not feeling at home with Jesus now, you won't want to be with Him when He returns. But if Jesus is at home with you now, you'll be at home with Him when He returns—you won't be "left behind."

So if you're not feeling at home with Jesus now, you won't want to be with Him when He returns. But if Jesus is at home with you now, you'll be at home with Him when He returns—you won't be "left behind."

What About the Millennium?

THERE IS A
RESURRECTION OF
THOSE WHO LIVE
AND REIGN WITH
CHRIST. IT'S
CALLED "THE
FIRST
RESURRECTION."

(REVELATION 20:5, 6)

Question: *What's the "millennium"? What will happen then, and why is it important?*

Answer: *The word "millennium" never appears in the Bible. It comes from the Latin words mille, meaning 1,000, and annus, which means years. (The Bible wasn't written in Latin, but it was later translated into Latin.)*

The only presentation of the millennium, or 1,000 years, in the Bible is in Revelation 20. There is obviously a lead-up to it that you can read about in Revelation 19. And there's a follow-up to it that's spelled out in Revelation 21.

Revelation 20 is quite a chapter! It tells of Satan's end, which is huge! And since Revelation 20 is in the symbolic book of Revelation, you can expect that different people are likely to have different interpretations.

The most frequently asked questions about the millennium are:

What will happen at the start of the 1,000 years?

What will happen at the end of the 1,000 years?

What will happen in between those two points in time?

I'll tease you with one questionable idea about the millennium. If the book of Revelation is symbolic, then what does the number 1,000 symbolize? A literal interpretation would be 1,000 actual years. A symbolic interpretation would take the number 10, which symbolizes completeness, and make it threefold (10 x 10 x 10 = 1,000). That could symbolize a trinity of completeness. In other words, this is the ultimate wrap-up, the completion of the plan of salvation.

When the millennium starts:

According to Revelation 19:11-21, the great controversy between Christ and Satan and their followers is coming to a climactic end! Even though it looks as though Satan will win (Revelation 12:17; 13:1-18), eventually he is defeated, and his followers die (Revelation 19:17-21). Then Satan is left on a desolate earth with nobody to tempt or to deceive (Revelation 20:1-3).

There is a resurrection of those who live and reign with Christ. It's called "the first resurrection" (Revelation 20:5, 6). According to 1 Thessalonians 4:15-18, when Jesus comes, He will raise all the "dead in Christ." Then Jesus will take to heaven those who were "dead in Christ" and His followers who are alive at that time. So here's what happens at the start of the millennium:

1. When Jesus comes, He resurrects the "dead in Christ" (this is "the first resurrection") and takes them to heaven (1 Thessalonians 4:16; Revelation 20:5, 6).

2. When Jesus comes, He also takes to heaven His followers who are alive at that time (1 Thessalonians 4:17).

3. When Jesus comes, those who are not followers of Jesus die (Revelation 19:21).

4. Satan is left on a desolate earth for the millennium (Revelation 20:1, 2).

What happens during the millennium:

Revelation 20:1-7 describes Satan as bound to earth, not because there's a large ball and chain around his ankle, but because there are no people for him to tempt or to deceive. The planet has been pretty much wiped out since the seven plagues have already fallen (Revelation 15, 16).

While Satan is bound to earth, the followers of Jesus—those He resurrected and those who were alive when Jesus came—are now in heaven. Revelation 20:4-6 says that they are seated on thrones, and they are judging.

During this time God's people will be able to ask God all their questions and get answers from Him, including why certain people are in heaven, and why others aren't. Lots of things we don't know about or understand right now will finally become clear to us then! This is a key reason why the millennium is so important—God wants to make everything clear to us, since we're going to spend eternity with Him!

Not only are God's people in heaven, but they are priests, and they reign with Christ (Revelation 20:6). I don't know if you're into power, majesty, and intimacy with God, but you get all of that by being a follower of Jesus. You might miss out on some of it now, but you won't during the millennium!

So here's what will go on during the millennium:

1. Satan is stuck on earth with nobody to tempt or to deceive—talk about the most boring time of his existence (Revelation 20:1-3)!

2. God's people get to ask God all of their questions, and He will answer them, including questions about how He's dealt with everyone on earth (Revelation 20:4-6).

3. God's people reign with Christ (Revelation 20:6).

When the millennium ends:

Revelation 20:7-15 describes what happens at the end of the millennium. Satan is set free from his prison, and he immediately goes out to deceive the nations from every corner of the earth. Evidently the people who aren't in heaven with Jesus are resurrected at the end of the 1,000 years. Revelation 20:6 alludes to this resurrection by pointing out what a blessing it is to be part of the first resurrection that took place at the start of the millennium, because "the second death has no power over them."

You'd think that all of these people who are part of the second resurrection would get a clue that they don't have a chance. But the Bible says that Satan deceives them, and that's not the first time he's done it! So they decide to try to overtake God and His people in God's city. But fire comes down from heaven and consumes them (Revelation 20:9, 10, 14, 15).

Just a quick word about the term "for ever and ever." It's a term that can mean for your whole life. When applied to God, it means forever, because He lives forever. When applied to humans, it's limited to however long their life is. So when the devil, the beast, and the false prophet (symbols of the powers associated with Satan) are thrown into the lake of fire where they burn "for ever and ever" (Revelation 20:10), it doesn't mean that for eternity there will be a fire of hell burning in a corner of the universe. At the end of the 1,000 years Satan and everything having to do with sin and death will be completely burned up (Malachi 4:1). That's the final end (Revelation 21:4).

Some people think that God is mean to resurrect those who aren't on His side just to destroy them in the lake of fire at the end (Revelation 20:7-15). But such a perspective fails to see that the core of God isn't pain or revenge, but fairness. In the book *The Great Controversy* on pages 666-673 is a fascinating description of what happens at the end of the millennium. A panoramic view of the history of this world reveals to all, including Satan, that God has been fair and full of mercy. Even Satan bends the knee to God (Philippians 2:10, 11).

God doesn't resurrect the wicked because He wants to kill them again. He resurrects them because He wants everyone to get the whole picture of the great controversy and His plan of redemption. This is His universe, and He wants to clear the record for everyone, including those who despise Him.

Then things get really happy. What happens after the millennium is spelled out in Revelation 21. This chapter is worth reading and imagining—it causes people to get giddy about heaven! So just to recap, here's what happens at the end of the millennium:

1. Those who didn't follow Jesus are resurrected (Revelation 20:7, 8).

2. Satan deceives these people (Revelation 20:8).

3. Satan and his followers try to destroy God and His people (Revelation 20:9).

4. Fire destroys Satan, his followers, and sin and death forever (Revelation 20:9-15).

5. The New Jerusalem comes to earth, where God dwells with His people (Revelation 21).

You asked why the millennium is important. It's part of the culmination of the end of death and sin and Satan, which completes God's plan of redemption. But the millennium itself points out that God wants to take time to answer everyone's questions about everything.

Right now there are times when things don't seem fair, and there are lots of pieces of information that we just don't know yet. Why does a baby die? Why do bad things happen to good people? Why do the wicked prosper? Why do natural disasters ruin God's creation? Why doesn't God intervene at times when it seems like He should? The millennium is the time when God will answer all of those questions, which is a very important time to God, and to us.

I'm looking forward to the millennium. How about you?

What About the 144,000?

"THEN I LOOKED,

AND THERE

BEFORE ME WAS

THE LAMB,

STANDING ON

MOUNT ZION,

AND WITH HIM

144,000 WHO

HAD HIS NAME

AND HIS FATHER'S

NAME WRITTEN

ON THEIR

FOREHEADS."

(REVELATION 14:1)

Question: *Who are the 144,000 people that the Bible talks about in Revelation?*

Answer: *Some people argue about this with intense passion. The number 144,000 appears only a few times in the Bible. But since it's from the book of Revelation, plenty of mystery and interpretations surround it.*

Let's read the passages that you're referring to from the Bible: "Then I heard the number of those who were sealed: 144,000 from all the tribes of Israel" (Revelation 7:4).

"Then I looked, and there before me was the Lamb, standing on Mount Zion, and with him 144,000 who had his name and his Father's name written on their foreheads" (Revelation 14:1).

139

"And they sang a new song before the throne and before the four living creatures and the elders. No one could learn the song except the 144,000 who had been redeemed from the earth. These are those who did not defile themselves with women, for they kept themselves pure. They follow the Lamb wherever he goes. They were purchased from among men and offered as firstfruits to God and the Lamb. No lie was found in their mouths; they are blameless" (Revelation 14:3-5).

That's it! Do you think you have enough information to answer your own question now? Reading the context of the passages (a few verses before and after them) can help. But it still might not make it crystal clear who the 144,000 are. From what we read they seem to be special people who are on God's side, maybe something like special Navy Seals or Army Rangers. Perhaps they are the few; the proud; the Marines—on God's side, of course!

Before taking any more stabs at what this number might mean, a burning question for those interested in the 144,000 often comes out as "Is the number 144,000 a literal number or a symbolic number?"

In most parts of the Bible you should expect things to be just as they are stated rather than turning them into something symbolic. For example, when Jesus said, "Love your enemies," He actually meant "love your enemies" (Matthew 5:44). That may be difficult, but the message is pretty straightforward. In Scripture there are some exceptions, but usually it literally means just what you read.

But when you read something from the book of Revelation or portions of Daniel or Ezekiel, you should expect it to be symbolic. A beast coming out of the water (in John's vision in Revelation 13) is probably symbolic rather than a new video game.

Based on that, if the 144,000 are described only in the book of Revelation, you should expect it to be a symbolic number. Indeed, the number 12 is the symbolic number for God's kingdom (12 tribes, 12 apostles, the foundation of the New Jerusalem has 12 different types of stones, the city is 12,000 stadia long, 12,000 wide and 12,000 tall, there are 12 gates to the city, etc.). You don't have to be a math genius to recognize that 12 times 12 equals 144! That's the kingdom number repeated (12 x 12). You'll find that same number is used to describe the width of the walls of the New Jerusalem (see Revelation 21).

The number 10 is used to symbolize completeness (such as 10 fingers and 10 toes are complete—nothing missing). If you multiply the number 10 x 10 x 10 again, you get 1,000. The number 3 symbolizes unity (like the trinity, the demonic trinity of dragon and beast and false prophet, the "holy, holy, holy" worship of God, etc.). So the number 1,000 means complete unity or a unity of completeness.

If you combine these symbols, the number 144,000 would be God's complete and unified kingdom. Want to be part of the 144,000? I sure do!

The 144,000 are in heaven, standing before God!

By the way, a similar type of marking was described in Ezekiel 9:4 for those in the earthly Jerusalem who were not part of the rebellion against God at that time. In Revelation the mark is placed on those in the New Jerusalem who are faithful to God. This is in contrast to those who receive the "mark" of the beast (see Revelation 13:16).

Notice these characteristics of the 144,000 in Revelation 14:

1. They sing a new song. Some see this as an allusion to the new song God's people sang after Moses led them through the Red Sea away from their powerful enemy, Pharaoh (see Exodus 15).

2. They have been redeemed from the earth. They are in heaven, so there's no question that these are God's people.

3. They have kept themselves pure from women. A problem with God's people has been sexual impurity, whether it was with the golden calf, the Moabite women after Balaam's curse didn't work, or as in the story of Hosea. Sexual infidelity became the symbol of unfaithfulness to God (see Revelation 17:1-5).

4. The 144,000 follow the Lamb wherever He goes. These people actually constantly follow Jesus.

5. The 144,000 were purchased and offered as firstfruits. Satan has no rights over these people. They have been bought back from sin, thanks to Jesus' sacrifice and His forgiveness and grace. The firstfruits were presented to God at each of the major Jewish festivals. They were the first in terms of either coming first timewise, or else they were first in terms of being the best. Some think these "firstfruits" come before a bunch of other redeemed people. Perhaps these people are those who are alive when Jesus returns. But there's a vast multitude that is also resurrected, so I don't think this is clear either way (Revelation 7:9).

6. No lie was found in their mouth; they are blameless. In contrast to David's words, "There is no one who does good" (Psalm 53:1), the 144,000 have been completely transformed. They evidently are living out the Beatitudes of Jesus (see Matthew 5:3-12).

Some people think that God's people have it good! These are probably the same type of people who expected Jesus to come as a king 2,000 years ago. Sometimes extreme difficulty comes before the reward. But the book of Revelation does describe the time when Jesus will return as King of kings. His people will be part of that celebration—the 144,000 are special!

If you had been racing into the Red Sea because Pharaoh was bearing down on you, it might not have seemed to be good to be part of God's people. Maybe it seems to you like people who enjoy the pleasures of sin on this earth don't get their fair consequences. Maybe you feel that following Jesus leaves you feeling left out of some activities and some friendships.

From what I read about the 144,000, this group of people is completely devoted to God, and theirs is an absolutely incredible reward. Count me in! How about you?

What About Seven Being the "Perfect" Number?

I'VE HEARD

PEOPLE REFER TO

THE NUMBER

"SEVEN" AS THE

SYMBOL OF

PERFECTION, BUT

I DON'T KNOW

HOW THEY CAME

UP WITH THAT

STATEMENT, MADE

SORT OF IN

PASSING AS IF

"EVERYONE

KNOWS THAT!"

Question: *Why is the number seven considered the "perfect" number in the Bible?*

Answer: *Where did you hear that "seven" is the perfect number? There certainly isn't a verse in the Bible that says, "Seven is the perfect number (and don't you ever forget it!)."*

I've heard people refer to the number "seven" as the symbol of perfection, but I don't know how they came up with that statement, made sort of in passing as if "everyone knows that!"

Perhaps it's based on the 7-day creation story in Genesis when the world was made perfect prior to sin entering it. Maybe it's based on all of the references to "seven" in the book of Revelation (7 candlesticks, 7 churches, 7 seals, 7 trumpets, 7 last plagues, etc.) Or maybe it's because Jesus told his disciples to forgive people not just 7 times, but "seventy times seven (70 x 7 – see Matthew 18:22).

Or maybe it's because some people get very creative with numbers. Let me give you some examples.

Did you know that the Hebrew word for "seven" occurs a total of 392 times in the Bible. Now this is absolutely amazing because 392 isn't just any number! No, it's actually a multiple of seven (7 x 7 x 8 = 392). But that's not all! The number 392 is also the sum of the square of seven (7 x 7 = 49) and the cube of seven (7 x 7 x 7 = 343) (49 + 343 = 392 which is how many times the Hebrew number "seven" appears in the Bible. Isn't that just "perfect"?

And did you know that the word "seven" appears exactly "seven" times in Genesis chapter seven?! Isn't that "perfect," too?!

And there's more! Sometimes the word "seven" is used more than once in the same verse. That means that of the 392 uses in the Hebrew Bible, there are less than 392 verses where you will find the word. You've got to be wondering how many verses have the word "seven" in them. Okay, I'll tell you. You'll find the number "seven" in 343 verses. And you know what that means, don't you? Yes, that's right (you're following me, aren't you?). The number 343 comes from 7 x 7 x 7 = 343! "Perfect" again!

And that's just the Old Testament (Hebrew Bible)! In the New Testament, the word "seven" and derivatives of it ("seventy" and "seventh") add up to 105 uses, and everyone knows that 105 is 3 x 5 x 7! Are you seeing the pattern? Of course, 3, 5, and 7 are the first three prime numbers (after 1 and 2), which keeps the perfect pattern going!

If this makes sense to you, I'm glad (because it doesn't make one bit of sense to me!). Oh, I understand the numbers; but I don't know what that has to do with being "perfect." I'd call it interesting, but not "perfect." We don't believe in "verbal inspiration" anyway, so what difference does the number of times seven shows up in Genesis 7 make any difference? Besides, chapter and verse divisions took place hundreds of years after the Bible was written in the first place.

But if number games fascinate you, then take this into consideration: the Bible I'm using right now to respond to this question comes from the "seventh" column in my bookcase, and it is the "seventh" Bible from the end. Not only that, but the last verse I looked up was on page 979 in that particular Bible! That means that the digit "7" was right in the middle, and flanked by a "9" on either side, and "9" is three times three, and the trinity is "three," so God has this number surrounded in my study right now! PERFECT!!!

According to *The Seventh-day Adventist Bible Commentary,* the number "seven" signifies fullness or completeness (sometimes "complete" is also considered "perfect"). Creation is the first use of seven. The Sabbath each week since creation keeps the number alive. The major Jewish feasts lasted for seven days. Priestly purification lasted for seven days, as did purification following leprosy or other unclean elements. Many of the symbols in the sanctuary utilized the number seven (seven-branch candlestick, blood sprinkled seven times on the Day of Atonement, circumcision came seven days after birth, sacrificial animals had to be at least seven days old, etc.).

The repetition of the number seven leads many to believe that it must be more than a coincidence. "Complete" might be a better understanding than "perfect" since the number is also attached to plagues and beastly heads and beastly horns.

Some people are really into "numerology" (the study of the symbolic meaning of numbers). It's probably obvious that I'm not. But here's what one of my seminary professors taught me about the symbolic meaning of numbers:

1 = wholeness (Monotheistic God – Deuteronomy 6:4)

3 = unity (Father, Son and Holy Spirit – John 14:16-18, 23, 26)

4 = worldwide (4 corners of the earth – Revelation 14:6)

6 = falling short of rest (towards the end of Creation – Exodus 20:9)

7 = rest (end of Creation – Genesis 2:1-3) OR complete (same as 10)

10 = complete (the entire group – Revelation 17:3, 12, 16)

12 = kingdom (tribes of Israel, New Jerusalem – Revelation 21:12, 14)

Most of the books of the Bible are not symbolic. The ones that are really stand out, such as Daniel and Revelation. But Ezekiel is also very symbolic. And the imagery in Revelation draws on other Old Testament books as well.

I would crown Revelation as the most symbolic book in the entire Bible. Look at what you can do with some of its numbers:

Notice all of the 12's in Revelation 21 when it comes to describing the New Jerusalem – 12 gates, 12 angels, 12 tribes of Israel, 12 foundation stones, 12 apostles, measurement in stadia 12 times 1,000, 12 squared cubits, 12 gems, 12 pearls.

And how about the number of inhabitants – 144,000 – which factors into 12 x 12 x 10 x 10 x 10. Symbolically that means kingdom x kingdom x complete x complete x complete. The three (unity) "completes" mean a unified completeness. In other words, the 144,000 is not a literal number, but the completely unified people of God in His kingdom.

On the negative side, the dragon, the beast, and false prophet of Revelation form a unity (three of them) against God. But despite that unity, they are unable to overcome God. Even the mark of the beast is the unity number 666 – unity in falling short of the rest only God provides.

Why is the number seven considered the perfect number in the Bible? I think it represents completeness (the full week of Creation) more than the slippery synonym "perfect." And I think we prefer the meaning "perfect" because that's what we desire for ourselves. But we can "rest" in God's "completeness" at all times and celebrate it every seven days (Sabbath) just as God does.

What About Homosexuality?

"IF A MAN LIES WITH A MAN AS ONE LIES WITH A WOMAN, BOTH OF THEM HAVE DONE WHAT IS DETESTABLE. THEY MUST BE PUT TO DEATH; THEIR BLOOD WILL BE ON THEIR OWN HEADS."

(LEVITICUS 20:13)

Question: *I have some gay friends, and all through the Bible it seems homosexuals get a bad rap— like they're going to hell for being gay. Why? I'm not gay, but I care about my friends. What can I tell them?*

Answer: *Homosexuality is a controversial topic.*

Some people are clearly on the anti-homosexual bandwagon for religious reasons, because homosexuality disgusts them, or because they fear homosexuality.

Not everyone is opposed to it, though. An increasing number of gay people are "coming out of the closet." Those who support them do so because they're pro-homosexuality, or they think people should be free to do whatever they want, especially if that's their choice or orientation. Some people even promote the Gay Pride movement.

There's controversy over homosexuality because people have opinions on opposite sides, and they discuss it more openly now than in the past. Also, let me point out that considering the topic of homosexuality is easier when you discuss it theoretically. Once you know people who are homosexual, it tends to change one's ideas from being theoretical (ideas only) to practical (what do we do now?).

For example, I might think homosexuality is bad—wrong, ungodly, unnatural, etc. Then I meet a wonderful person who becomes my friend. After we become friends, I find out he's gay. How do I relate to him? Here are four possible options:

1. Relate to him the same way I did before. (Ignore my thoughts about homosexuality being bad.)

2. Be repulsed and draw away or persecute the gay person. (Since homosexuality is bad, I treat the homosexual in a bad way.)

3. Be repulsed and try to correct my gay friend. (Since homosexuality is bad, and since you are my friend, I will help you turn away from homosexuality.)

4. Adjust my conviction that homosexuality is bad, since my friend isn't a bad person.

Although these are some natural reactions, as Christians we want to live for Jesus, and we get our instruction and clues from the Bible, not merely circumstances that come our way. So what does the Bible say about homosexuality? Here are a few texts people turn to when considering this topic:

"Do not lie with a man as one lies with a woman; that is detestable" (Leviticus 18:22).

"If a man lies with a man as one lies with a woman, both of them have done what is detestable. They must be put to death; their blood will be on their own heads" (Leviticus 20:13).

"Because of this [trading the truth of God for a lie], God gave them over to shameful lusts. Even their women exchanged natural relations for unnatural ones. In the same way the men also abandoned natural relations with women and were inflamed with lust for one another. Men committed indecent acts with other men, and received in themselves the due penalty for their perversion" (Romans 1:26, 27).

"Surely you know that the people who do wrong will not inherit God's kingdom. Do not be fooled. Those who sin sexually, worship idols, take part in adultery, those who are male prostitutes, or men who have sexual relations with other men, those who steal, are greedy, get drunk, lie about others, or rob—these people will not inherit God's kingdom. In the past, some of you were like that, but you were washed clean. You were made holy, and you were made right with God in the name of the Lord Jesus Christ and in the Spirit of our God" (1 Corinthians 6:9, 10, NCV).

"But we know that the law is good if someone uses it lawfully. We also know that the law is not made for good people but for those who are against the law and for those who refuse to follow it. It is for people who are against God and are sinful, who are not holy and have no religion, who kill their fathers and mothers, who murder, who take part in sexual sins, who have sexual relations with people of the same sex, who sell slaves, who tell lies, who speak falsely, and who do anything against the true teaching of God" (1 Timothy 1:8-10, NCV).

For many, reading these five passages provides a quick and conclusive answer to your question. According to the Bible, homosexuality is bad. The reason homosexuality gets a "bad rap" is that it's sin.

In our society today there's been an increasing awareness and acceptance of homosexuality. The media presents it in more positive or neutral stances than in the past. And behavioral sciences are now suggesting that homosexuality can be either a person's right to choose or an orientation with which they're born.

Our current culture doesn't consider the Bible a source of authority. But as Christians, we desire to follow what God has revealed in the Bible. We live in our culture sometimes as "pilgrims and strangers" in anticipation of heaven. (See Ellen G. White's book *Early Writings*, p. 113.)

In recent years some who study the Bible have sought to find a greater openness to homosexuality. They've wondered, Is it possible that our reading of Scripture in the past has given us a bias against homosexuality? If a person is gay, do they have to turn their back on who they are? Or is the only other option to turn one's back on God and the Bible?

For a pro-homosexual understanding of Scripture, you'll somehow have to explain away the texts already presented. Here's how some people have done it.

They say that the two passages from Leviticus are simply for the Jewish people in Old Testament times, so we can throw those out with the ceremonial laws about sacrificing animals.

Then they say that the three passages written by Paul aren't about homosexuality as we know it today. Paul was referring to old men having sex with young boys (pedophilia). So homosexuality is fine. It's pedophilia that's bad.

You might hear of the term "sodomy" as males having sex with males, perhaps in a raping fashion. The term comes from the biblical story of what happened in Sodom when God sent angels to warn Lot and his family about Sodom's imminent destruction and the men of the city wanted to have sex with the male visitors (Genesis 19:1-5). Sodom was soon destroyed, and this male gang raping seems to be the lightning rod of all that was bad in Sodom.

Pro-homosexuality Christians have said that the sin of Sodom wasn't sexual—it was lacking hospitality for the strangers who came into the city that evening. For evidence in Scripture, they point to Ezekiel 16:48 and 49, but leave out verse 50. I think these attempts to explain away the texts that straightforwardly condemn homosexuality are rather flimsy.

But how should we relate to homosexuals in a culture that's quick to support their freedom of sexual expression. Is homosexuality any worse than the other sins it sometimes gets listed with in the Bible (refer back to 1 Corinthians 6:9-10 and 1 Timothy 1:8-10 above)? Or should we just look the other way, as we tend to do sometimes with lying, petty thievery, or greed?

"Sin" is no longer a politically correct topic. But as Christians, sin is a reality we must deal with. Drop the "tendency" and "orientation" smooth talk—as in "I have a tendency to lose my temper" or "My orientation is to be loyal to family no matter what." We need to come to the realization that we naturally sin, and we choose to. Another way to state it is that we're naturally selfish.

Some argue that since that's the way we are naturally, that's not "good" or "bad"; it just "is." I disagree (see Romans 3:23). It's very bad! When I do even good things, it can be for bad motives. I can manipulate, humiliate, alter the truth, and do whatever else I need to do in order to come out on top, or at least look out for myself.

I can do this even in religious circles. Why? It comes to me "naturally." But all of this is "bad," even if others might congratulate me on my skill, my drive, or my achievements.

How does this relate to homosexuality? If a person is born with a homosexual orientation, that doesn't make it right. If I'm born with a promiscuous orientation (I want to have sex with as many people of the opposite gender as I possibly can), that doesn't make it right either. If I'm born with a very strong desire and even a talent for stealing, that doesn't make stealing right for me.

It seems to me that the sexual orientation argument is a nice way of saying, "This is what I want; therefore, this is what I get." That approach sounds like basic selfishness to me, whether it's about sex, money, power, or some other topic.

Paul talks about crucifying and dying to one's sinful nature. That's because each one of us is naturally selfish. Here's how Galatians 2:20 reads: "I have been crucified with Christ: and I myself no longer live, but Christ lives in me. And the real life I now have within this body is a result of my trusting in the Son of God, who loved me and gave himself for me"(TLB).

Once we come to the realization that we're naturally selfish and sinful, the response God looks for in us is admitting it (acknowledging it); asking for the gift of repentance (being sorry); and then asking Him for a new life (help to go in the opposite direction you've been heading). Those who take pride in what comes naturally to them seem clueless that God desires so much more—see Ephesians 3:20.

And that's not the end of it. Paul also alerted us to the need to actively choose the new life instead of the old, naturally selfish life. According to Romans 8:12-14: "So, dear brothers, you have no obligation whatever to your old sinful nature to do what it begs you to do. For if you keep on following it you are lost and will perish, but if through the power of the Holy Spirit you crush it and its evil deeds, you shall live. For all who are led by the Spirit of God are sons of God" (TLB).

These passages are about all types of sin, preferences, orientations, etc., not merely homosexuality. When a person states that homosexuality is wrong, a defensive reaction would be, "Well, the Bible also mentions greed and lying in the same list as homosexuality."

My response would be "Indeed! Greed and lying need to be crushed, too! Since all have sinned, we're all in this together. Let's not pass over or ignore homosexuality just because we don't want to get rid of greed or lying as our favorite sins."

When God created the first humans, he created male and female to complete His image (see Genesis 1:27). I can't find any place in Scripture where God created, condoned, or simply didn't care about homosexuality. Those who suggest David and Jonathan had a homosexual relationship have nothing to base it on besides their own creative thinking.

And just as God created us as sexual beings, Satan has sought to undermine and distort this gift. The results have been disastrous! Our human race suffers major deterioration, partly because of the misuse and abuse of our sexuality. In Romans 1 you can find Paul's illustration of just how far we've gone away from God's intention. Three verses deal with a variety of sins (29-31); and four verses deal specifically with the misuse of one's sexuality (24-27).

I think God's gift of sexual expression has become a key point of Satan's attack through perversion, re-imaging, and misrepresentation. God's intention that sexual expression be the crowning point of selflessness has been replaced with sex as the starting point for selfishness.

Does this mean that a person who's a homosexual is lost? Yes, just like a thief, liar, greedy person, drunkard, and others are lost. All are in need of cleansing and reorientation that only Jesus can provide.

Does this mean that after a simple prayer, your impulses and desires will change? Some people can answer yes. Others have to answer no. But if you pray this prayer and you don't feel a change in your orientation or desires, what does change is that God's Spirit comes to live within you to give you power to live differently.

I don't expect it to be easy, just as it isn't easy for a single male or female who's 28 and unmarried to be sexually pure. But that's what I believe God chooses for them and will give them the power to do. Just as a murderer, glutton, or liar might still murder, overeat, or lie, that's not something to celebrate. It's something to confess, repent of, and start overcoming again.

Does homosexuality get a bum rap in Scripture? I certainly think so. In fact, all sin does. Does this mean you shouldn't be friends with homosexuals? Of course you should. I would suggest that you be friends with homosexuals, greedy people, envious people, and even depraved people, and offer to pray for God's activity in their lives.

And one more thing—ask them to pray for God's activity in your life in areas that are "natural" to you but aren't godly. You need the same grace from God as they do.

Let's keep going to God for His grace instead of standing up for our own natural sinfulness and calling it "good."

And just as God created us as sexual beings, Satan has sought to undermine and distort this gift.

What About All of the Killing in the Bible?

SO WHY IS THERE
SO MUCH KILLING
IN THE BIBLE?
BECAUSE THERE IS
SO MUCH
REBELLION
AGAINST GOD.

Question: *Why is there so much killing in the Bible?*

Answer: *The Bible could be rated "R" for violence. From Genesis to Revelation you can find story after story about people killing one another even though the sixth commandment reads, "Thou shalt not kill" (Exodus 20:13, KJV).*

So why is there so much killing in the Bible? Because there is so much rebellion against God. Clear back in the Garden of Eden God warned Adam and Eve to obey Him rather than to rebel, otherwise they'd die (Genesis 2:17).

It sounds absolutely absurd, but humans who receive life from God will end up dying and/or killing each other when they rebel against God, their source of life (Genesis 2:7). It's a form of suicide, yet people continue to do it! Isn't it amazing that so many people in rebellion against God continue to be oblivious to the fact that it's the goodness of God that sustains them, even while they rebel (Matthew 5:45)?

God really is merciful. In the Bible when entire groups of people got killed via God's orders, as brutal as it sounds, God had already given these people years—often centuries—to get their lives back on track with Him. Instead, they persisted in their rebellion. For example, God gave the Amalekites 400 years to turn their lives around. Talk about being stuck in a rut!

You can find another example of God's grace in action in His instructions to the Israelites after He freed them from slavery in Egypt. God's retaliation rules mercifully went against current custom. In Exodus 21:24, 25 you can read about an "eye for eye" and a "tooth for tooth," etc.

At that time if you poked out one of my eyes, current custom dictated that I could poke out both of your eyes. And if you knocked out one of my teeth, I could knock out 10 of yours to teach you a lesson.

Trying to shape His people to be more merciful than those around them, Jesus took retaliation to another level. He said to "turn the other cheek" instead of repaying an "eye for eye" and "tooth for tooth" (Matthew 5:38-42).

The real reason there's so much killing in the Bible is that the Bible records the stories of God and His people on a planet in rebellion. But let's up the stakes even higher!

The two largest massacres spoken of in the Bible originate with God. The first one already happened—the Flood (Genesis 6-8). Only Noah and his immediate family survived, even though everyone received an invitation to enter the ark Noah built so they could be saved. (Those are very important points to remember.)

The second massacre will take place in the future in the lake of fire that consumes all who aren't with Jesus at the end of the millennium—1,000 years after He comes a second time and takes His followers to heaven.

(An important point to remember is that everyone receives an invitation to go to heaven with Jesus.) Then Jesus will bring His followers back to earth and set up a New Jerusalem on a clean earth (Revelation 20:7-9; 21:1-4).

I could actually respond to your question with a counter question: "Why is there so much living in the Bible?" People would've wiped each other out long before now if God hadn't intervened and provided life even for those in rebellion. There's God's mercy at work again.

To help us understand how we should act during this great war between good and evil on planet earth, Jesus said, "The thief's purpose is to steal and kill and destroy. My purpose is to give life in all its fullness" (John 10:10, NLT). His followers do the same, taking life to so many on a planet full of killing, until He remodels earth and makes it new.

"The thief's purpose is to steal and kill and destroy. My purpose is to give life in all its fullness."

(John 10:10, NLT)

What About Getting the Animals into Noah's Ark?

"YOU ARE TO BRING INTO THE ARK TWO OF ALL LIVING CREATURES, MALE AND FEMALE, TO KEEP THEM ALIVE WITH YOU. TWO OF EVERY KIND OF BIRD, OF EVERY KIND OF ANIMAL AND OF EVERY KIND OF CREATURE THAT MOVES ALONG THE GROUND WILL COME TO YOU TO BE KEPT ALIVE."

(GENESIS 6:19, 20)

Question: *How did Noah get every animal to go into the ark?*

Answer: *I think he had a bunch of M&M's, and they ate their way into the ark! Naw, that's probably not right. Let me try another explanation.*

While cutting down trees in the forest for the ark, Noah learned how to become a lion tamer, which came in handy . . . No, I don't think that was it.

Maybe he was a "horse-whisperer" kind of guy and just talked the animals' language.

Let's try to find an answer in the Bible instead of in my creative ramblings. You can find the story in Genesis 6 and 7. Here are a few of the key verses:

"You are to bring into the ark two of all living creatures, male and female, to keep them alive with you. Two of every kind of bird, of every kind of animal and of every kind of creature that moves along the ground will come to you to be kept alive" (Genesis 6:19, 20). Notice that it says the creatures "will come to you."

"Pairs of clean and unclean animals, of birds and of all creatures that move along the ground, male and female, came to Noah and entered the ark, as God had commanded Noah. And after the seven days the floodwaters came on the earth" (Genesis 7:8-10). Notice again that the animals came to Noah, and this happened seven days before it even began to rain.

So how did Noah get every single animal into the ark? The Bible doesn't seem to give much of an answer. It just says the animals came to him—including the birds!

To see if I could find out more, I checked out two different Bible commentaries. They were written by scholars who've spent most of their lives studying the Bible. Checking them often provides helpful insight. But both of them had absolutely nothing to say about these verses. They talk in detail about the verses around them, including how important the detailed dimensions of the ark were. But neither commentary had anything to say about the animals. I don't think these scholars know either.

Next I checked in with a prophet that I believe received messages from God for us. She wrote a number of books about the Bible and about practical living for Christians. Here's what I found in the book *Patriarchs and Prophets*, by Ellen White on pages 97 and 98:

> "Now the servant of God [Noah] made his last solemn appeal to the people. With an agony of desire that words cannot express, he entreated them to seek a refuge while it might be found. Again they rejected his words, and raised their voices in jest and scoffing. Suddenly a silence fell upon the mocking throng. Beasts of every description, the fiercest as well as the most gentle, were seen coming from mountain and forest and quietly making their way toward the ark. A noise as of a rushing wind was heard, and lo, birds were flocking from all directions, their numbers darkening the heavens, and in perfect order they passed to the ark. Animals

obeyed the command of God, while men were disobedient. Guided by holy angels, they 'went in two and two unto Noah into the ark,' and the clean beasts by sevens. The world looked on in wonder, some in fear. Philosophers were called upon to account for the singular occurrence, but in vain. It was a mystery which they could not fathom. But men had become so hardened by their persistent rejection of light that even this scene produced but a momentary impression."

If you want a short answer, it's in that paragraph: the animals obeyed the command of God and were guided by holy angels. I recommend that you read the entire chapter in *Patriarchs and Prophets* called "The Flood," pages 90-104.

I can't help thinking of the words of Jesus, "As it was in the days of Noah, so it will be at the coming of the Son of Man" (Matthew 24:37). Read "The Flood" in *Patriarchs and Prophets*, and then compare it to what life is like today. You'll be glad that the same angels are available to help you obey the commands of God and guide you just as they did the animals.

If you want a short answer, it's in that paragraph: the animals obeyed the command of God and were guided by holy angels.

What About Women Who Defy God?

"A WOMAN MUST
NOT WEAR MEN'S
CLOTHING, NOR A
MAN WEAR
WOMEN'S
CLOTHING, FOR
THE LORD YOUR
GOD DETESTS
ANYONE WHO
DOES THIS."

(DEUTERONOMY 22:5)

Question: *As I was studying the Bible, I came across Deuteronomy 22:5. I'm wondering, Why do most women defy God's Word?*

Answer: *I'm delighted to hear that you've been studying the Bible. It often leads to a closer relationship with Jesus.*

Y*ou specifically mentioned Deuteronomy 22:5, which reads, "A woman must not wear men's clothing, nor a man wear women's clothing, for the Lord your God detests anyone who does this."*

Now let me try to answer your question. Most women violate God's Word because they're selfish. The Bible describes it this way: "You want something but don't get it. You kill and covet, but you cannot have what you want. You quarrel and fight. You do not have, because you do not ask God. When you ask, you do not receive, because you ask with wrong motives, that you may spend what you get on your pleasures. You adulterous people, don't you know that friendship with the world is hatred toward God? Anyone who chooses to be a friend of the world becomes an enemy of God" (James 4:2-4).

So there's your answer. But before you share this with all the women you know, go back and read everything above again. God's Word mentioned both women and men in Deuteronomy 22:5. I think that both women and men are naturally very selfish, which leads them to defy God's Word.

But what does that have to do with a woman wearing pants or a man having long hair? People often use this text to hammer people that they think are going against God by wearing the current style.

For example, when I was a teen, long hair for guys was in. Some people would use Deuteronomy 22:5 to "prove" that God was opposed to long hair on guys. Then some guy would pull out an artist's rendering of Jesus with long hair.

Somebody else would denounce females for wearing pants instead of a skirt or dress. Then somebody would pull out a picture of a male wearing a skirt, like the Scottish kilt that bagpipers wear.

If you travel outside of the U.S., you're apt to see women wearing "men's" clothing and men wearing "women's" clothing. This is called culture shock, not violating God's Word. I haven't been to that many countries, but I've seen males in India wearing skirts and males in Guatemala wearing very short skirts.

So what does Deuteronomy 22:5 really mean? I suggest you check out a Bible commentary when you come to things like this that make you wonder. Or you can ask others, like you did in this case.

When I looked up Deuteronomy 22:5 in the *Seventh-day Adventist Bible Commentary*, it explained that this verse is talking about people—women and men—who cross-dress for immoral sexual reasons.

God created males and females in His image, with the ability to be intimate with one another within the security of marital commitment. Cross-dressing for immoral sex certainly misses that mark. No wonder God is against it, for women as well as for men.

God created males and females in His image, with the ability to be intimate with one another within the security of marital commitment.

What About a Sanctuary in Heaven?

Question: *What's Jesus doing in the sanctuary in heaven right now?*

Answer: *When you talk about a sanctuary in heaven, I'm guessing that you're probably a Seventh-day Adventist. Most Christians haven't even heard of a heavenly sanctuary—and many Adventist teens haven't either.*

L*et's start with the first earthly sanctuary. After delivering His people from Egyptian slavery, God took them to Mount Sinai. There He spoke and wrote the Ten Commandments for them, while He met directly with Moses for more than a month. One of the things God shared with Moses during this time was a complete plan for a sanctuary. He said,*

"Have them make a sanctuary for me, and I will dwell among them" (Exodus 25:8).

The whole purpose of the sanctuary was for God to be right in the middle of His people. That's difficult when You're divine and sinless, and You want to be in the middle of created beings who are sinful. See, God's passion for us continues even though our passion for Him fluctuates.

The book of Hebrews points out how Jesus is the focal point of everything God gave to the Hebrews. This includes the sanctuary, the priesthood, the high priest, the law, faith, angels, the Sabbath, and Moses.

One verse in Hebrews gives a quick answer to your question. It's found in Hebrews 7:25, and it says, "He is able to save completely those who come to God through him, because he always lives to intercede for them."

The key word is "intercede." It's what you do when you speak up for somebody. If your friend is in trouble with somebody, you may want to put yourself on the line for your friend. Some people do this with just a word or two. Others really get into it. And some even get physical!

So what does it mean that Jesus "always lives to intercede for them"? The "them" is us. We've already mentioned what "intercede" means. The phrase "always lives" is very important, too. In Old Testament times you can imagine how good it was to have a priest who knew you to be the one who interceded for you. When the priest died, you'd have a new priest who may not know you, and it would be like starting over. But in Hebrews we find that Jesus "always lives," which means we can count on Him! We don't have to wonder or worry about who might replace Him someday.

Sometimes the word "intercede" carries along with it some negative images. There have been times when I pictured a court scene in which Satan is the prosecuting attorney (see Revelation 12:10 for a reference about the "accuser"), and Jesus is my defense attorney. I imagine God the Father as the judge.

When Satan makes his accusations against me in that court scene, he may lie if he wants to. But I realize that there are enough things I'm ashamed of and guilty of that he doesn't really need to lie to do me in. So my hope is that somehow Jesus will magically pull me out of my guiltiness or get Satan on some technicality.

That's where God's forgiveness and Jesus' death give me a clean slate. But in the back of my head, I sometimes wonder if Jesus might get tired of my inconsistent life, or if maybe God the Father figures that enough people have been given grace, and it's time for me to get what I deserve instead of what I don't deserve. What will the verdict be? Is Jesus really "interceding" for me?

If you ever get a warped view of God like this, check out Romans 8:26, 27, which says, "The Holy Spirit helps us in our distress. For we don't even know what we should pray for, nor how we should pray. But the Holy Spirit prays for us with groanings that cannot be expressed in words. And the Father who knows all hearts knows what the Spirit is saying, for the Spirit pleads for us believers in harmony with God's own will" (NLT).

So not only is Jesus interceding for us, but so is the Holy Spirit. And the Father gets into it by getting on the same wavelength as the Spirit. If you want a fuller understanding of this, read Romans 8:31-39. The final lines of this passage summarize what God the Father thinks of us: "Nothing in all creation will ever be able to separate us from the love of God that is revealed in Christ Jesus our Lord" (NLT).

What is Jesus doing in heaven right now? According to John 14:2, He is preparing a room for us in His Father's house. The reason Jesus is doing this isn't merely to build up His Father's property. In John 14:3 He explained why He's doing this: "So that you will always be with me where I am." It's all about being together. Right now Jesus, God, and the Holy Spirit are working everything out so that we can be with Them forever.

Since Jesus "has your back" (and your front), you can chill about this whole fight between good and evil that takes place in our world, as well as in our individual lives. God calls "chilling" rest. He takes the metaphor of the Sabbath and says it doesn't have to be only one day each week; it can be the lifestyle of the believer when they've put everything in His hands (see Hebrews 4:9, 10).

Hebrews 4 ends this way: "That is why we have a great High Priest who has gone to heaven, Jesus the Son of God. Let us cling to him and never stop trusting him. This High Priest of ours understands our weaknesses, for he faced all of the same temptations we do, yet he did not sin. So let us come boldly to the throne of our gracious God. There we will receive his mercy, and we will find grace to help us when we need it" (verses 14-16) (NLT).

"Nothing in all creation will ever be able to separate us from the love of God that is revealed in Christ Jesus our Lord." Romans 8:31-39 (NLT)

Questions About the Church

- A Reason to Go to Church?
- Not Feeling Welcomed at Church?
- Going Back to Church?
- Finding the True Denomination?
- SDA's Being a Cult?
- Who Started the SDA Church?
- Holding My Youth Group Together?
- Becoming a Pastor?
- Female Pasters?
- Ordaining Women?
- Ellen White?
- Ellen White Being "Inspired"?
- God's Final Church?

What About A Reason to Go to Church?

Question: *I'm bored at church. I know you're going to say I should keep going, but why?*

Answer: *First of all, I'm not going to say that you should keep going. But I will tell you a few things that might sound as if that's what I'm saying.*

Instead, *why don't you try going to church for the first time? What I mean by that is to go with everything that you have, not just walk into a building and plop down on a pew. Get involved!*

Jesus quoted the Old Testament prophet Isaiah (is that boring?) when He said, "These people honor me with their lips, but their hearts are far away. Their worship is a farce, for they replace God's commands with their own man-made teachings" (Matthew 15:8, 9, NLT).

Here were people who lacked life because they were just going through the motions. Jesus called such worship "a farce." The same kind of thing can be true today. So, instead of just doing the same ol' thing at church, try giving it all you've got.

What I'm getting at is that worship takes everything you have; it's a total involvement experience. If you treat it like a form of entertainment, where you can channel surf or switch to a new Internet site or tune out with your iPod or some other form of escape, you're missing what worship is about.

When Jesus interacted with the Samaritan woman at Jacob's well, she asked Him about going to the right place for church. She wondered why the Jews insisted on Jerusalem, while the Samaritans chose another spot, Mount Gerizim. Jesus told her, "The time is coming and is already here when true worshipers will worship the Father in spirit and in truth. The Father is looking for anyone who will worship him that way. For God is Spirit, so those who worship him must worship in spirit and in truth" (John 4:23, 24, NLT).

Boredom isn't the issue! It's not a matter of "Hey, I'm bored; I think I'll quit." The thing that counts is getting your spirit—your inner core, who you really are, the deepest part of you—into contact with the Source of Life for the Universe. So here are two ways to do that.

1. **Ask yourself.** Do I go to church to be entertained, or to worship the Spirit with my spirit? You won't be able to do both. Another way of asking the same question is, Do you go to church to get something, or to give something? Ironically, if you go to get something, you probably won't get it! Yet, if you go to *give* something, you end up getting it!

2. **Get involved.** That's what it takes for your spirit to worship. If a person prays out loud for the congregation, and you don't understand what the person's talking about, or if they take too long, add your silent prayer to this prayer time. If the Scripture reading makes no sense to you, read the verses before and after it. And then read the passage again (and again, and again). If the music isn't a style you prefer, broaden your tastes instead of

scowling and withdrawing. When the pastor preaches, focus on what's being said. Your mind can think faster than a person can talk, so as you focus, add all kinds of thoughts, questions, interpretations, prayers, and answers to what the preacher says.

You can worship all by yourself rather than during a regular church service. But there's something extra to worship when more people get involved and with their spirits also worship the Spirit. If you can get a bunch of your friends to join you by getting involved at a worship session at your church, great things can happen!

But if you just go to church to hang out with friends, you might as well be watching a video or DVD of some TV preacher. You can eat popcorn, talk with your friends, or even be bored. But you won't be worshipping.

What I'm getting at is that worship takes everything you have; it's a total involvement experience.

What About Not Feeling Welcomed at Church?

I DON'T FEEL WELCOME AT MY CHURCH. THE PEOPLE ARE STUCK UP, AND I DON'T LIKE STUCK-UP PEOPLE. I KNOW THAT I SHOULD TALK TO MY PASTOR ABOUT THIS, BUT I DON'T KNOW WHAT TO SAY.

Question: *I don't feel welcome at my church. The people are stuck up, and I don't like stuck-up people. I know that I should talk to my pastor about this, but I don't know what to say.*

Answer: *It's absolutely horrible not to feel welcome at your own church! I know that churches often emphasize the need and desire to be friendly, but that doesn't always make them friendly.*

P*robably about the time you were just a child, I worked on a study of Adventist churches and found that most teens didn't feel as though their churches were "warm and accepting." It's a big problem! It seems*

171

there could be several reasons the people at your church aren't friendly.

1. They simply aren't friendly.

2. They're hurting, and they need somebody to be friendly to them.

3. They're friendly but only to certain people.

4. They don't know what to say to you.

5. They're intimidated by you. (Surprisingly, many adults are intimidated by teens.)

You could probably come up with other reasons. I'm just pointing out things I've noticed and reasons people have shared with me. Now, what can you do about it?

1. Initiate conversations with others in your church. According to Proverbs 18:24: "A man that hath friends must shew himself friendly" (KJV).

2. Take this chapter in the book to your pastor and ask if s/he thinks unfriendliness is a problem in your church.

3. Sit by someone in your church who seems stuck up, then pray for something to talk about with them. Don't get up without saying something to them, even if you just ask to borrow their bulletin for a moment.

4. Act as if you're taking a survey. Ask members to rate your church's friendliness on a scale of 1 (low) to 10 (high). Then ask them why they rate it that way.

5. Hold up a large sign that reads "I need somebody to talk to me." Then time how long it takes for somebody to respond.

6. Announce in your church bulletin that there's a mystery person in your congregation who has a special secret, but people have to ask around to find out who the mystery person is—you. What's the secret? You haven't found people to be friendly in your church.

Ask if that is a secret to anyone else.

7. Ask the pastor if you can do the scripture reading some Sabbath. When you get up front, tell people you're nervous and ask them to tell you how you did.

8. Ask the pastor if you can be a "greeter"—one of those people who hands out bulletins and welcomes people to church. It will force you to talk to other people. (Even stuck-up people want a church bulletin.)

9. Help in one of the children's Sabbath school divisions at your church. Children are often more outgoing than adults.

10. Here are a couple lines you could use on the people in your church who seem stuck up: How long have you been attending this church? How did you become an Adventist?

I can't think of anyone who likes stuck-up people. So get unstuck from this bad situation yourself, and maybe some of the others won't be stuck up anymore either.

I can't think of anyone who likes stuck-up people. So get unstuck from this bad situation yourself, and maybe some of the others won't be stuck up anymore either.

What About Going Back to a Church?

IF PEOPLE I DIDN'T REALLY KNOW AT A CHURCH TOLD ME THAT I WASN'T WELCOME, I'D FIND IT VERY DIFFICULT TO GO BACK.

Question: *My friend has gone to church only a couple of times, because when he went, the people there told him he wasn't welcome. Then his parents told him he wasn't good enough for church. He really feels hurt. My question is "Should he go back to church?"*

Answer: *If people I didn't really know at a church told me that I wasn't welcome, I'd find it very difficult to go back. And if my parents told me that I wasn't good enough for church, I think I'd get defensive, and I'd feel hurt, too.*

I *wonder why your friend went to church in the first place. Did you invite your friend to go to church? Did your friend go out of curiosity? Or out of a desire to please somebody? Was your friend trying to make a scene, searching for God, doing a report for a class, checking out the opposite sex, wanting a place to pray, or hanging with friends? What's the story?*

I can't help thinking about something similar that happened in the days of Jesus. Here's how it's recorded in Matthew 9:10-13:

"While Jesus was having a meal in Matthew's house, many tax collectors and other outcasts came and joined Jesus and his disciples at the table. Some Pharisees saw this and asked his disciples, 'Why does your teacher eat with such people?'

"Jesus heard them and answered, 'People who are well do not need a doctor, but only those who are sick. Go and find out what is meant by the Scripture that says: "It is kindness that I want, not animal sacrifices." I have not come to call respectable people, but outcasts'" (TEV).

Sound like the same type of thing? I've heard it said that our church is a hospital for sinners, not a hotel for saints. That means that your friend is always welcomed by God to visit His house.

But when your friend gets to God's house—or hospital—he or she might not see the Physician or nurses or even a receptionist. Your friend very well may see other patients!

If you were bleeding to death or had some broken bones and you went to the hospital emergency room, how would you feel if a person whose right arm had just been amputated came to you first? And then what if a person with a gunshot wound to the face cut in front of you?

Sometimes wounded people can feel your pain, because they share a similar type of pain. Sometimes wounded people can even heal you. But most people want to see a physician rather than other patients—at least if they're hurt!

So when you see other hurt people at church, you can understand why they're present—they want to be healed too. No wonder Jesus said, "Come to me, all of you who are tired from carrying heavy loads, and I will give you rest. Take my yoke and put it on you, and learn from me, because I am gentle and humble in spirit; and you will find rest. For the yoke I will give you is easy, and the load I will put on you is light" (Matthew 11:28-30, TEV).

In the meantime, yes, your friend should go back to church. Go with your friend. Introduce your friend to those who can help your friend get well. And maybe you and your friend can help some of the other patients at church be healed too!

"Come to me, all of you who are tired from carrying heavy loads, and I will give you rest. Take my yoke and put it on you, and learn from me, because I am gentle and humble in spirit; and you will find rest. For the yoke I will give you is easy, and the load I will put on you is light." (Matthew 11:28-30, TEV)

What About Finding the True Denomination?

Question: *Which religion/ denomination is the true one?*

Answer: *That's a simple question for me. The true religion/ denomination is ours, right?*

Most religions/denominations believe that they are the "true" one. The reasons vary, but it usually comes down to one of the following foundations:

1. God says we're right—it says so in the Bible.

2. We have a history of God's activity with us.

3. Something supernatural got us going.

4. Everyone else is off; we've got it right.

In the United States about 150 years ago when the Seventh-day Adventist Church got started, people's mind-set at the time was to find "truth" in the Bible. It was common to have public debates and to argue for hours. Seventh-day Adventists tended to do fairly well in such debates.

But the mind-set in the United States is quite different now. At the present time, people value openness and consider multiple answers as all possibly right. Even partially right answers are considered good; while zeroing in on only one "true answer" is thought to be too narrow-minded.

I've found that many teens who've grown up as Seventh-day Adventists want to find out how solid Seventh-day Adventist beliefs are before they make a full commitment to the religion/denomination. Sometimes they want to check out other denominations or religions and maybe experiment for a while.

I want to encourage you to be a "God-seeker" and to continue to search for a greater understanding of God, a broadening appreciation for God, and a deeper intimacy with Him. If the religion/denomination you're a part of doesn't lead you in these ways, what's it doing?

The Seventh-day Adventist Church has a published set of official beliefs. But the church is more than just beliefs. The people and the mission of the church are also important elements to consider. Allow me to focus on one element for a moment—the *introduction* to the beliefs of the Seventh-day Adventist Church as of this moment:

"Seventh-day Adventists accept the Bible as their only creed and hold certain fundamental beliefs to be the teaching of the Holy Scriptures. These beliefs, as set forth here, constitute the church's understanding and expression of the teaching of Scripture. Revision of these statements may be expected at a General Conference session when the church is led by the Holy Spirit to a fuller understanding of Bible truth or finds better language in which to express the teachings of God's Holy Word."

For a description of each belief of the Seventh-day Adventist Church, go to www.adventist.org/beliefs/fundamental/index.html.

I believe each of the Seventh-day Adventist Church's fundamental beliefs. I also get excited about our introduction for two reasons: because the Bible is our source of authority, not one person or a committee; and because we can expect the Holy Spirit to continue to lead us to revise our understanding of God.

Are you open to that? Do you expect it? Or are you set in stone, and there's nothing more for God to share with you?

I was born into the Seventh-day Adventist religion, because my parents are both Seventh-day Adventists. I chose to be a Seventh-day Adventist during my teen years. As an adult, there have been times when I disagreed with a few of the beliefs or the way some of the beliefs were presented or emphasized. I've considered other religions and have found some items to be attractive and other parts to be equally or more repulsive than some of the hang-ups I've had in Adventism.

Here's what I can say to you: please keep searching for God yourself. When you consider the Seventh-day Adventist beliefs, look at each one and ask, "What does this tell me about Jesus?"

I've found that each belief of the Seventh-day Adventist Church gives me a special perspective on Jesus, sort of like looking at a large jewel from many different angles. Right now I'm appreciating the way the light catches it from so many vantage points, and I'm loving Jesus more and more.

Please keep searching for God yourself. When you consider the Seventh-day Adventist beliefs, look at each one and ask, "What does this tell me about Jesus?"

What About SDAs Being a Cult?

PERHAPS THE WORST ASSOCIATION WITH THE WORD "CULT" BRINGS TO MIND A GROUP OF WEIRDOS WHO FOLLOW SOME CHARISMATIC LEADER AND DO THINGS THAT SEEM BIZARRE TO MOST PEOPLE.

Question: *Why do some people think that the Seventh-day Adventist Church is a cult?*

Answer: *Probably because the Seventh-day Adventist Church is a cult! There, do I have your attention?*

The word "cult" literally means "worship," and that worship is usually a worship of the deity. So yes, Seventh-day Adventists worship the Deity, as do all other Christians. In fact, people in other world religions and even pagans worship what they consider to be deity/gods, whether it's the sun, moon, rain, crops, or ancestors whom they believe are more powerful than people living on earth today.

But the word "cult" also brings to mind other meanings. In a larger context, Christians are a cult in the country of India, where the majority of people are Hindus. But Hindus are a cult in the United States, where the majority of people are Christians.

Small, more recent religious groups are considered to be cults if they aren't part of the mainstream. Jehovah's Witnesses, Latter-day Saints, (sometimes called Mormons), and Seventh-day Adventists sometimes get classified as cults.

Perhaps the worst association with the word "cult" brings to mind a group of weirdos who follow some charismatic leader and do things that seem bizarre to most people. The key leader becomes as a god to these people who might be manipulated in a number of ways. Full commitment to the leader is necessary, and followers often give them their commitment when the leader is perceived as a type of god or hero.

For many Christians the negative use of the term "cult" refers to a distortion of the basic beliefs of Christianity, such as the Bible, the Trinity, and salvation by grace through faith.

About 50 years ago Walter Martin wrote a book called *The Kingdom of the Cults*. In his book Martin identified Seventh-day Adventists as one of the cults that claims to be Christian but really isn't. The distortions he identified included:

1. Salvation resulting from obeying the Ten Commandments (including the fourth commandment about the Sabbath).

2. The writings of Ellen White being more important than the Bible to Seventh-day Adventists.

The Seventh-day Adventist Church published a book in response to Walter Martin's assertions, called *Seventh-day Adventists Answer Questions on Doctrine*. In it Adventists point out that we believe salvation comes only by grace—a gift from God through faith, by trusting Jesus for everything; and the writings of Ellen White are good for helping people understand the Bible, but they are not as important as the Bible! By the way, this book was reprinted in 2003 and edited by George Knight.

When Walter Martin revised his book, he wrote that he had made a mistake about Seventh-day Adventists, and that they really are true Christians.

If you read the first edition of *The Kingdom of the Cults*, you may think that Seventh-day Adventists are a cult in the negative sense of the term. If you know of Seventh-day Adventists who think that salvation comes from something they do instead of as a gift from God, you'd find some people who claim to be Adventists, but they don't really believe what Adventists officially believe!

I've met a few Seventh-day Adventists who appreciate the writings of Ellen White so much that they seem to follow them more than the Bible. That sounds like a cult to me.

How about you? Do you follow distortions of Christianity? Do you even know what the basic beliefs of Christians are? Are you more apt to follow these beliefs too much or too little? Do you worship, since that's what the word "cult" actually means?

In it Adventists point out that we believe salvation comes only by grace—a gift from God through faith, by trusting Jesus for everything; and the writings of Ellen White are good for helping people understand the Bible, but they are not as important as the Bible!

What About Who Started the SDA Church?

THEY CAME TO THE POINT OF EMPHASIZING "PRESENT TRUTH," WHICH WAS TRUTH ESPECIALLY IMPORTANT AT THE PRESENT TIME. AS A RESULT, THEY WERE OFTEN IN THE THICK OF THINGS AROUND THEM, BECAUSE THEY LIVED IN THE PRESENT TENSE.

Question: *Who started Seventh-day Adventism?*

Answer: *If you're interested in an online, official answer, check out www.adventist.org. Then select "world church" from the navigation bar. In the menu underneath "world church," click on "facts and figures," then click on "history."*

Here's my answer: *God started Seventh-day Adventism through a group of young people in the northeastern United States in the 1840s.*

There's much more to the story. If you like history, there are actually plenty of stories about the start of Adventism. Most of the young people were already Christians. Many of them were kicked out of their churches because they were quite passionate about the "advent," the coming of Christ. Why? Their enthusiasm annoyed the people in their old churches; it rocked their boat of comfortable Christianity.

While the majority of the people who started the Seventh-day Adventist Church were young people, older people were instrumental in providing wisdom and encouragement. These passionate people studied the Bible and experienced strong convictions about what they found. They didn't always agree, but they continued to study. Some of their conclusions turned out to be wrong. So they had to admit their mistakes and study some more.

They came to the point of emphasizing "present truth," which was truth especially important at the present time. As a result, they were often in the thick of things around them, because they lived in the present tense.

If you want some key names for the start of Seventh-day Adventism, they would include William Miller, Josiah Litch, Charles Fitch, Joshua Himes, Joseph Bates, Frederick Wheeler, Hiram Edson, Ellen Harmon-White, James White, John Andrews, Uriah Smith, Stephen Haskell, and John Loughborough. The names continued to grow as the years went by. It wasn't just one person who charismatically led a bunch of people.

Anyway, this bunch of people clustered around a message about the return of Jesus, the Advent. Later they found the Sabbath to be a forgotten gift and a call from God. By 1863, after much wrestling with the idea of starting a new denomination, they formed the Seventh-day Adventist Church. They did so primarily for organizational reasons, even though some feared that by forming a denomination, they'd lose their passion for Christ. That's what they'd seen happen in so many denominations around them.

For more than 150 years there have been changes in the Seventh-day Adventist Church. The vast majority of the denomination is made up of young people, although that's not true in Western countries such as Europe, Australia, Canada, and the United States, which all together comprise less than 10 percent of the Adventists in the world.

Most of the action in the Adventist Church still comes from young people. If you go to Africa or Latin America or even Asia, it's the young people who continue to spread "present truth." And it's in these countries that the majority of Seventh-day Adventists live today.

There are a few pockets of action among young people in the Western world, but not many. The time is ripe for a new revolution of young people to be active in their world for Jesus, rather than playing church on weekends and living for themselves all week. There's a need to give up the pleasures, vices, and enticements of the world and to commit to taking Jesus into every place and to every person in the world.

When young people do that, they're living like the young people who started Seventh-day Adventism instead of like the people who got annoyed with them when they rocked the boat at their nice, complacent churches.

Where are you when it comes to Seventh-day Adventism? Are you passionate about Jesus' advent? Or are you part of the status quo?

There's a need to give up the pleasures, vices, and enticements of the world and to commit to taking Jesus into every place and to every person in the world.

What About Holding My Youth Group Together?

"MY GOD WILL

MEET ALL YOUR

NEEDS

ACCORDING TO

HIS GLORIOUS

RICHES IN CHRIST

JESUS."

(PHILIPPIANS 4:19)

Question: *My youth group is falling apart. We used to be close and have some great student leaders. But most of them graduated this past year, and now the group is a mess.*

I graduate this coming spring, and I'm afraid nothing will be around for the younger kids when they hit the youth group. What can I do to help right now?

Answer: *It sounds as if you're in a major crisis. Sometimes people do crazy, reactionary things when they feel this kind of pressure. But sometimes people really get motivated to do positive things. And often this is the time you see God's work, because you're desperate for a miracle!*

Don't fall into the trap of thinking that everything depends on you for your youth ministry (or any ministry, for that matter). Yes, you can get busy, expecting God to sprinkle your ideas with blessings and provide enough people to make it worth your effort.

But for ministry to happen, you need God. The human part (that's you) can go through the motions, but what you really want is for God to be present and real in what happens.

We often apply Philippians 4:19 to individuals, but actually this passage was written to the entire church in Philippi. It says, "My God will meet all your needs according to his glorious riches in Christ Jesus."

God has chosen to work through humans in all kinds of ways. To me that's an incredible miracle! It creates purpose in my life, compassion for others, a desire to share my faith, and encounters of experiencing God. I can't think of much that can beat that!

But you're in a crisis mode with your youth group. So let me point out two dynamics that might be happening.

1. **Youth groups go through cycles. You mentioned that the youth who graduated this past year were the key leaders. Since their absence nothing seems to be happening.**

When a group of strong leaders graduates, there's bound to be a vacuum. This provides an opportunity for new leaders to take over and develop.

Usually this takes some time, though. Probably those who graduated started off a bit rough, but by the time they graduated they'd developed to the point of proficiency.

Some youth groups anticipate this and keep training leaders of all ages all the time. But you still experience a difference simply because some clumps of people leave and others (usually much younger and less mature) join. You can figure on a major transition at the start and/or end of each school year.

Some grades seem to have lots of strong leader types and others don't. Certain grades are more spiritually oriented than others. So expect variety rather than everything staying the same.

2. **Let go of "the good ol' days." We humans tend to remember in glowing terms what things used to be like. For instance, when you were younger you probably looked up to the youth who were a few years older than you and who provided lots of leadership.**

Guess what? They probably looked up to other youth leaders who were gone by the time you joined the group. And don't be surprised if the younger youth look to you as a leader and have no recollection of those great leaders from past years.

This happened in Old Testament times. Some of the older people who came back from captivity saw the Temple being built. According to Ezra 3:12, "many of the older priests and Levites and family heads, who had seen the former temple, wept aloud when they saw the foundation of this temple being laid, while many others shouted for joy."

The younger people rejoiced to have a temple. The older people lamented that it wasn't like the one they remembered from years ago. So my message to you is: "Let it go!"

Now, how do you cope? First, thank God for what you experienced in the past. Then be sure to place the present and the future in His hands. That means you'll need to trust Him to take care of your group.

How can you help? Share your concerns with other current youth leaders, and invite them to pray with you. Then watch for indications of what God wants to do with and through your youth group.

Look for younger leaders who can start functioning in leadership roles. After all, you'll soon be gone too. And remember, God is the consistent presence in ministering through all kinds of young people as they pass through the youth group.

One other thing—if you never grow out of youth group ministry, you could become a youth pastor!

One other thing—if you never grow out of youth group ministry, you could become a youth pastor!

What About Becoming a Pastor?

ARE YOU A
FOLLOWER OF
JESUS?

WHAT HAS GOD
ALREADY EQUIPPED
YOU TO DO THAT
HELPS OTHERS?

WHAT ARE YOU
DOING TO MINISTER
TO PEOPLE RIGHT
NOW?

WHAT TYPES OF
SERVICE BRING JOY
TO YOU?

WHAT FEEDBACK
DO YOU GET FROM
OTHER FOLLOWERS
OF JESUS
REGARDING YOUR
SERVICE?

Question: *Lately I've been feeling impressed to go into the ministry, but I want to know for sure if I should become a pastor. How can I know?*

Answer: *I asked myself that same question before I became a pastor, and even after I became one. The most frequent advice people gave me was on the topic of talents and trying them out in pastoral activities.*

I've heard of schools that support "shadowing" programs in which students follow somebody in their job for a day, sort of like being in that person's shadow. If you did that, you'd get a better idea of what the "job" is really like, not just what you see on Sabbath morning.

If you do, you may find yourself visiting people in the hospital, answering the phone, trying to get the church copy machine fixed immediately, giving a Bible study, stopping by to sort clothing with the Community Services retirees, sitting through a committee meeting, going through mail, listening to complaints, brainstorming how to share the gospel, scrubbing toilets, visiting somebody in jail, traveling a half hour to an appointment and having the person not show up, sharing your faith while you wait in line at the post office, or leading a prayer group. Then you might get a chance to squeeze in lunch as you prepare for the afternoon!

In the Old Testament you'll find God calling prophets like Samuel (1 Samuel 3:1-16) and Isaiah (Isaiah 6:1-8). He also called family leaders like Abraham (Genesis 12:1-3) and Jacob (Genesis 28:10-15; 32:22-28). He revealed Himself to Daniel (Daniel 2:19) and asked Ezekiel to do some odd things (Ezekiel 5:1-6; 12:3-7).

In the New Testament God changed His plan as to how to reach all people with His good news. Instead of revealing Himself to the Israelites and blessing everyone through them, God showed Himself in Jesus. Now He's reaching all people through followers of Jesus. It's in this context that you'll discover the concept that all God's followers are "ministers," using the talents God's given them to minister to others.

Here are a few questions I have for you:

- Are you a follower of Jesus?

- What has God already equipped you to do that helps others?

- What are you doing to minister to people right now?

- What types of service bring joy to you?

- What feedback do you get from other followers of Jesus regarding your service?

You can want to be a pastor, but it's God who gives people the various types of gifts to serve Him. According to Ephesians 4:11-13, "it was he who gave some to be apostles, some to be prophets, some to be evangelists, and some to be pastors and teachers, to prepare God's people for works of service, so that the body of Christ may be built up until we all reach unity in the faith and in the knowledge of the Son of God and become mature, attaining to the whole measure of the fullness of Christ."

If you want to find out if God is calling you to minister as a pastor, talk to your own pastor about it, start doing the types of things pastors do, and pray for God to give you gifts, or to lead you to discover other ways you can "minister" for Him.

If you want to find out if God is calling you to minister as a pastor, talk to your own pastor about it, start doing the types of things pastors do, and pray for God to give you gifts, or to lead you to discover other ways you can "minister" for Him.

What About Female Pastors?

IF YOU'RE A FEMALE WHO'S CONSIDERING WHETHER OR NOT GOD IS CALLING YOU TO BE A PASTOR, THIS BECOMES A VITAL QUESTION.

Question: *What does the Bible have to say about women pastors?*

Answer: *Nothing specific. That's why so many people have come up with their own opinions. Books have been written to "prove" that women should be pastors, and other books have been written to "prove" that women should not be pastors. Both types of books claim that the Bible clearly reveals their position.*

When there are two sides to an issue, it's not surprising when teams arm for battle and take up the fight to win the war for their position. For those who don't really care about either side, the issue isn't worth their time and energy. So they drop out completely.

If you're a female who's considering whether or not God is calling you to be a pastor, this becomes a vital question. Would God give you impressions or a message to become a pastor when He doesn't actually want females to be pastors? If those impressions aren't from God, are they from Satan?

If you're a male, does this issue really matter? It doesn't if it's not about you. But if it's about you, it does matter, since males and females are in the debate. This isn't a fight among females only. Some males fear what might happen if females enter their sacred domain.

Here's one text from the Bible for either side.

Women shouldn't be pastors

The favorite text for this side is 1 Timothy 2:12, which says, "I do not permit a woman to teach or to have authority over a man; she must be silent." It sometimes gets paraphrased as "Women are to be silent in church."

The frequent association people make with a pastor is the preaching that takes place during the church worship service. Of course, pastors do many other things besides preach. However, this duty seems to be called into question for females.

A theme for this "side" is that God chose males to be spiritual leaders for His people—for example, Abraham, Isaac, and Jacob; Moses, Aaron, and Joshua. When God selected a priesthood, He chose the males from the tribe of Levi. When Jesus called His disciples, He selected males, not females. So why would God make a change now? And would God make such a change without letting us know?

Women should be pastors

A favorite text for this group is Galatians 3:27, 28, which says, "For all of you who were baptized into Christ have clothed yourselves with Christ. There is neither Jew nor Greek, slave nor free, male nor female, for you are all one in Christ Jesus." When you become a follower of Jesus, everything seems to change. Designations such as gender, race, nationality, economic status, popularity—all these things disintegrate when you give your life to Jesus.

The common theme used to support this position deals with spiritual gifts. Because God gives spiritual gifts to whomever God chooses, and because the gift of "pastor" is one of those gifts, being female doesn't disqualify you.

What am I to do?
At this point you may be wondering: When the Bible isn't clear about a topic, or when it seems to present support for opposite sides, what should a person do?

Here's what the early Adventists did. They got together and studied the Bible and prayed. Even though a female prophet was part of their group, she didn't give them the simple answer, because God hadn't given it to her.

After the group hammered out a belief, the prophet would receive a vision that confirmed their conclusion. This gave them courage to continue in their newfound understanding.

I suggest that you do the same thing. Get together with some people to study the Bible as a group. It might take several sessions. Pray. Look for confirmation from God. Use this chapter as a starting point, but there's much more to discover and discuss.

In my parents' generation, people weren't even expecting females to receive the gift of pastoring. In my generation we believe it is possible. And it seems to me that the current generation of young people expects God to give the gift to both males and females.

Because there seems to be some confusion about this question from the Bible, I've studied the topic by myself and with groups of people. And I've seen an increasing number of females who have been given the gift of pastoring.

As a Seventh-day Adventist Church we've voted that women cannot be ordained as pastors, but they can be hired as pastors. I think God has been giving the gift of pastoring to both females and males, but we're just starting to catch on to that reality.

What About Ordaining Women?

IF WOMEN CAN BE ORDAINED AS ELDERS, COULD THEY ALSO BE ORDAINED AS PASTORS?

Question: *Can or should women be ordained?*

Answer: *"Yes/No" and "it depends." Let me try to explain my answers.*

*C*an women be ordained? I said "Yes" because they have been, even in the Seventh-day Adventist Church. When I was a kid, women were not ordained. We ordained men—as pastors, as elders, and as deacons. But when a woman would become a deaconess, there was no ordination; they just did it.

Later I learned that the word "deacon," used during ordination services for deacons when the pastor would read from 1 Timothy 3:8-10, is the same word used for the female "deaconess" in Romans 16:1. That made me wonder why we "ordain" the males but not the females when it's the same word that is used in the Bible.

As an adult living in the United States I found myself in a sea of changing traditions. Males working outside of the home and females working inside of the home didn't describe everyone like it used to (and still do in many parts of the world). Women have always done significant service in churches, whether they are recognized for it or not.

The issue of females becoming elders created quite a stir in some congregations. People said things like, "It's time we make some changes around here and that includes making some women elders." Others said, "We've never done it that way and we're not about to change just because the world is doing things differently."

Church leaders discussed it and since elders and deacons are selected by individual churches, the organized church headquarters decided that each church should choose for itself whether or not a female could or should become an elder.

Not surprisingly, some churches voted to do it and some churches voted not to do it.

So, yes, women have been ordained as elders in Seventh-day Adventist churches, but certainly not every church.

You can probably anticipate what the next step would be. If women can be ordained as elders, could they also be ordained as pastors? In the Seventh-day Adventist Church, pastors are ordained by conferences, but even these must get approval from the next highest organizational group—the unions. Now, instead of one church voting whether or not a female could be ordained as a pastor, it is up to the conference and union—a group of pastors already ordained (so, that means that all of the ones who make the decision are males). It seemed like nobody wanted to deal with this political hot potato.

That's why the decision was taken to the highest organizational group in the Seventh-day Adventist Church. The General Conference session takes place every five years. In 1990, a much-anticipated request to ordain females as pastors came to the General Conference session. While church leaders from North America (less than 10% of the votes) requested that women be ordained as pastors, the majority of those represented were from Africa and Latin America. The majority voted against females being ordained as pastors. There were very strong feelings on both sides of the issue (I was there).

People from North America realized that where the majority of Adventists live in the world, having a female function in the role of a pastor was unthinkable. So, at the next General Conference session (1995), those from the North American Division requested that each division of the world church vote for itself on the issue (there are 11 divisions), not that every division should necessarily have female pastors.

Again, heated debate took place, not about each division choosing for itself, but about whether or not females should be ordained as pastors. Once again, the church seemed strongly opinionated on the topic (my wife was there). The majority voted against the proposal. According to the General Conference of Seventh-day Adventists, females cannot be ordained as pastors.

Since that time, a number of females have been "commissioned" as pastors in North America. This has turned out to be a way to not go against the decision that females cannot be "ordained," but it has opened the door for females to be recognized as pastors by substituting a different word.

You asked, "Should women be ordained?" Whether it's in the role of an elder or a pastor, I think the issue is the same—what does ordination mean?

If ordination means that a person is given unique, spiritual powers the moment ordination takes place, then whoever gets ordained will have those powers. You'll need to be very careful who you give those powers to. This is a Catholic view of ordination.

If ordination means that the church is simply acknowledging that a person is already functioning with unique, spiritual powers because the Holy Spirit has given them those powers, then God is the one who gives the power, not the church leaders. This is a Protestant view of ordination.

What do you think? Are you Catholic or Protestant? (Most Seventh-day Adventists consider themselves to be Protestants.) Do you believe that when church leaders pray a prayer and put their hands on the head or shoulders of a person, going through those motions gives the person unique, spiritual powers? Or do you believe that the Holy Spirit is the one who gives people the gifts the Holy Spirit chooses, and church leaders simply acknowledge what the Spirit has already done?

According to 1 Corinthians 12:11 (NLT), "It is the one and only Holy Spirit who distributes these gifts. He alone decides which gift each person should have." I think that churches should be on the lookout for the activity of the Spirit, and ordain those to whom the Holy Spirit has given the spiritual gift of being a pastor. If the Spirit has already done it, who are we to deny it? Let's celebrate and acknowledge what the Spirit has done!

"It is the one and only Holy Spirit who distributes these gifts. He alone decides which gift each person should have."

1 Corinthians 12:11 (NLT)

What About Ellen White?

ELLEN WHITE
CERTAINLY LED
PEOPLE TO JESUS
(THE BOOK STEPS
TO CHRIST HAS
BEEN TRANSLATED
INTO 140
LANGUAGES),
MOST OF THE
MINISTRY OF A
PROPHET IS TO
DELIVER MESSAGES
FROM GOD.

Question: *Who was Ellen White? It seems as if the most important person in the Catholic Church is Mary. Is Ellen White like Mary for the Seventh-day Adventist Church?*

Answer: *Ellen White was a human being who lived more than 100 years ago (1827-1915). She played an important role in the group of people who started the Seventh-day Adventist Church.*

I suppose that if the only thing you're considering is prominent females within a denomination, then Ellen White for SDAs and Mary (the mother of Jesus) for Catholics would be somewhat similar. But the details are quite different. Note these comparisons:

Ellen White

1. Lived in the nineteenth and twentieth centuries.

2. Lived in the United States, Europe, and Australia.

3. Helped start the Seventh-day Adventist Church.

4. Received the gift of prophecy, including dreams and visions, which provided messages from God to the early Adventist Church.

5. Gave birth to several boys, none of whom made any claims to be the Messiah. They tended to follow their mother's ministry rather than exceed it.

6. Wrote bunches of books and thousands of articles that are still read today.

7. Traveled extensively and spoke publicly.

Mary (the mother of Jesus)

1. Lived in the first century B.C. and the first century A.D.

2. Lived in Palestine.

3. Died long before the Catholic Church organized.

4. Showed no indication of the gift of prophecy and left no record of dreams or visions (although her husband received some—see Matthew 2:13, 19).

5. Gave birth to the Messiah.

6. Did not leave any written records that we know of.

7. Seemed to be a stay-at-home mom.

There's another major difference between the role of Ellen White and how people view Mary. Although Ellen White certainly led people to Jesus (the book *Steps to Christ* has been translated into 140 languages), most of the ministry of a prophet is to deliver messages from God. In contrast, people turn to Mary not to get a message from God, but to get a message to God.

This requires a belief that Mary is alive and in heaven, still functioning in a motherly fashion. It also includes a belief that Jesus is too busy to listen to our prayers or answer them in our favor, so perhaps Mary will convince Him to think positively toward us.

But this perspective doesn't fit the Bible. Mary isn't alive or living in heaven. And Jesus certainly has time for us and is very involved in our lives. In Luke 18:16 you can read about Jesus calling for children to come to Him when others thought He didn't have time for them. Jesus also spoke about being so involved in our lives that even the hairs on our head are numbered (Matthew 10:30). There's no need for an earthly mother to try to get the attention of Jesus for us. He's already focused on you.

If you'd like more information about Ellen White, check out the Web site: www.whiteestate.org.

There's no need for an earthly mother to try to get the attention of Jesus for us. He's already focused on you.

What About Ellen White Being "Inspired"?

BEING A PROPHET ISN'T ALWAYS A FUN TASK. SOMETIMES THE PEOPLE WHO RECEIVE THE MESSAGE TURN ON THE MESSENGER. SOMETIMES THEY LISTEN AND OBEY, BUT USUALLY THEY DON'T.

Question: *How do we know Ellen G. White was inspired by God? There were other people besides Bible authors who've been inspired by God, and we don't know about them.*

Answer: *First allow me to respond to your question, then I'd like to challenge you regarding your comment.*

Many people think Ellen White was just minding her own business and suddenly got zapped by God and started prophesying, sort of like King Saul in the Old Testament (see 1 Samuel 19:20, 24).

But the role of being a prophet is usually about passing along a message from God—simply being a conduit. If you have a brother or sister, you've probably been a "prophet" for your parents when you've said, "Mom says get off the computer now," or something like that.

Being a prophet isn't always a fun task. Sometimes the people who receive the message turn on the messenger. Sometimes they listen and obey, but usually they don't.

Ellen White provided two kinds of key messages for the early Adventist Church. One had to do with the beliefs we hold to be true. Now, you'd think that Ellen White would simply announce, "God says to believe _____" and that would be it.

Instead, the Adventist pioneers studied and discussed the Bible at great lengths. After they reached a conclusion, Ellen White would receive a vision that confirmed their conclusion. It was sort of like God was saying, "That's right; keep going!"

The second type of message Ellen White passed on to early Adventists was to give some general counsel to the church as a whole or to individuals or small groups in particular.

For example, most Adventists, including Ellen White, ate a somewhat unhealthy diet. Then God revealed in a vision to Ellen White that healthful living is part of His ideal for us. Ellen White passed along that message. It was difficult for some (including Ellen White—she was human, you know) to live it.

Ellen White also had some specific counsel for specific individuals. Sometimes these were for church leaders who weren't too interested in hearing a message from God, but she delivered it anyway. A collection of these can be found in the nine-volume set called *Testimonies* for the Church.

I recommend that you go to an Adventist Book Center or go to www.adventistbookcenter.com and check out some books George Knight has written about Ellen White.

What's surprising to me is that many Adventists these days have some definite opinions about Ellen White, but very few have read what she's written. I suggest you read her books *Steps to Christ, The Desire of Ages*, or

Patriarchs and Prophets. I also know people who've been very blessed by the new paraphrase of *The Desire of Ages* called *Messiah*.

Here's my challenge to you based on Joel 2:28, 29, which reads, "I will pour out my Spirit on all people. Your sons and daughters will prophesy, your old men will dream dreams, your young men will see visions. . . . I will pour out my Spirit in those days."

You can expect that God won't be silent. You should expect that many people will be passing along messages from God. And with that, you can expect that Satan will throw in his share of counterfeit messages, too.

Here are the main questions you should always ask: Is the message consistent with Jesus and with the Bible? Messages from God will be consistent with Jesus and Scripture. That underscores how important it is to be hooked in with Jesus and His Word.

By the way, if you're a Seventh-day Adventist, welcome to a people who've been called to be prophets as a group. We have a message to spread to the world. Are you one of the prophets, too?

Messages from God will be consistent with Jesus and Scripture. That underscores how important it is to be hooked in with Jesus and His Word.

What About God's Final Church?

SEVENTH-DAY
ADVENTISTS ARE
PART OF THE
PROTESTANT
MOVEMENT THAT
SEEKS GOD
DIRECTLY, NOT
THROUGH HUMAN
CHANNELS,
DECREES, OR
TRADITIONS.

Question: *Is the Seventh-day Adventist Church God's remnant, end-time people?*

Answer: *The word "remnant" means a lot to some people and absolutely nothing to others. The same is true about "end-time." Here's your question without those key words: Is the Seventh-day Adventist Church God's people? Let's respond to that question and then consider the other terms.*

I believe the Seventh-day Adventist Church is God's people. While we're not as old as many Protestant denominations, our roots go all the way back to God's call to Abram (later called Abraham) in Genesis 12.

God's call involved trusting Him in big things and little things, in fact, in all areas of life. It also included having an on-going relationship with Him. In return, God's desire was to bless His people so that they'd bless others. The blessings for others could be with material things or spiritual things.

But God's people didn't always maintain an on-going relationship with Him. Read the book of Judges or 2 Kings for more examples than you'll ever want to know! Yet God sent messengers called prophets to bring His people back to Him.

When that didn't work, He sent enemies that helped people sense their need for something greater than themselves and to receive the blessings like He'd given them previously. Read one of the many examples in 2 Chronicles 20:1-30.

Eventually God sent His Son, Jesus, to this earth, but God's people killed Him. Read about that in the form of a parable in Matthew 21:33-46. Now that's really messed up!

Just before He returned to heaven, Jesus told His disciples that they'd receive power when the Holy Spirit came upon them. That would lead to their witnessing where they were and eventually to the whole world. It did! Incredible things happened—read the whole book of Acts!

But eventually God's people slipped into following traditions and human explanations about God, so that they were actually following humans instead of God. Then there was a great movement to reform things. The reformers received the general term "protestant" because they "protested" what was going on in the church.

Seventh-day Adventists are part of the Protestant movement that seeks God directly, not through human channels, decrees, or traditions.

In the middle of Revelation God gives a warning message for all people throughout the world. It calls for us to return to God, our Creator. Seventh-day Adventists see this as our call to share the gospel of Jesus as Creator of the world and the Ten Commandments, namely the fourth commandment. Read Revelation 14:7.

Many Christians share Jesus with others. Seventh-day Adventists are Christians, so we do the same thing. Our unique understanding and contributions about Jesus include His promise to return and the gift of the Sabbath.

The context of time takes us back to those unique terms in your question: "remnant" and "end-time." You may have heard of carpet remnants or fabric remnants. It's the last bit on the roll or bolt when most of the material is gone. Sometimes there isn't enough left to be useful for much. It's usually reduced in price and doesn't amount to enough for a regular purchase. Sometimes it's just thrown away. It's the last you'll see of that item.

The word "remnant" can be found repeatedly in Isaiah and Jeremiah. See Isaiah 10:20-22; 11:11; 37:31, 32; 46:3 and Jeremiah 23:3; 31:7; 42:2; 43:5. It always refers to the last bit. Sometimes it's favorable, and sometimes it's not.

As Seventh-day Adventists, we believe that we are followers of Jesus. While it's a privileged role, we carry no status with it, and we're not the only ones. Read John 10:16! We're part of sharing the good news, not hoarding it! Since we believe we're living at the end of this world's history, yes, we're His "end-time" people. We're not many in number, but we are the last bit, the remnant.

Don't let this go to your head. Instead, let it go to your heart. Then, rather than falsely thinking you're better than others, you'll reach out and share the gospel so that others will be part of God's end-time, remnant people, just like you!

Since we believe we're living at the end of this world's history, yes, we're His "end-time" people.

Questions About Life

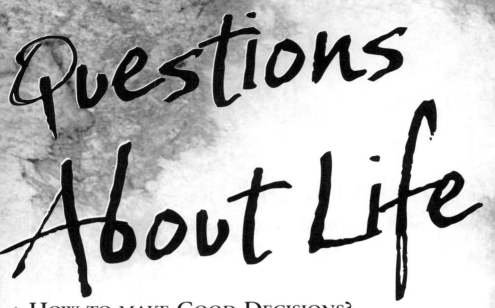

- How to make Good Decisions?
- Being Blessed?
- Being Called a Christian?
- Why Bad Things Happen?
- Anger—Is It a Sin?
- Killing When You're in the Military?
- Masturbation?
- My Mind Wandering When I Pray?
- Praying for Someone to Like Me?
- Getting Myself Organized?
- Academics at an Adventist School?
- Pets Going to Heaven?

What About How To Make Good Decisions?

I DON'T KNOW OF A PLACE IN THE BIBLE THAT SPECIFICALLY SAYS, "DECISION-MAKING: HOW TO DO IT IN 3 EASY STEPS."

Question: *Can you give me some biblical advice on how to make good decisions? It seems like I'm really good at making bad decisions, and I don't want to make any more bad decisions.*

Answer: *I recently asked a group of teens how they make decisions. Here's what they came up with on the spot:*

- Prayer
- Talk with people
- Friends
- Compare with my morals
- Very carefully
- Flip a coin
- Research it
- Experience
- I take the easy way

I don't know of a place in the Bible that specifically says, "Decision-making: How to do it in 3 easy steps." In fact, you may find some very different ways of making decisions recorded in the Bible, and some of them seem to be fine or even good as far as God is concerned. Check out these examples:

1. In Acts 1:15-26 you will find the story of selecting a twelfth disciple after Judas had committed suicide and Jesus had returned to heaven. There are several steps to this process. First of all Peter, one of the outspoken leaders, attributed the demise of Judas to an Old Testament prediction. Then he admonished the others to select a replacement based on experience—having been with the rest of the disciples from the baptism of Jesus until His ascension back to heaven. Nominations were made. (Sounds like a good democratic process, doesn't it?) Then they prayed for God to show them the one He wanted. (very spiritual, don't you think?) And then (you might find this hard to believe, but check Acts 1:26) THEY CAST LOTS! In other words, they just rolled the dice or drew a name out of the hat, and called that "The Will of God"!

2. The promise of Isaiah 30:21 sounds ideal for somebody who wants to follow God. Here's how it reads in the *New Living Translation,* "You will hear a voice say, 'This is the way; turn around and walk here.'" Wouldn't it be great to have God tell you what decision to make? Most of us would say, "Yes!:" unless God's instruction is different from what we want. If you read the rest of Isaiah 30, you'll find that God's people weren't listening too well to what God had already told them. In Isaiah 30:10 you'll find, "They [God's people] tell the prophets, 'Shut up! We don't want any more of your reports.' They say, 'Don't tell us the truth. Tell us nice things. Tell us lies.'" God warns them that they will get calamity and destruction as a result. But then God tells them that He will still come after His rebellious people, calling out to them, so they will hear a voice telling them what to do. That's quite a picture, isn't it?!

3. Here's one more "Biblical example." Check out the words of Jesus in Matthew 12:38-42. The religious leaders asked Jesus to give them a miraculous sign to show that He was from God. They claimed that their decision on whether or not to believe Jesus was based on a miraculous sign. Yet Jesus said they were part of an

"evil, faithless generation" because they asked for a miraculous sign. Then he told them something about Jonah being in the belly of the great fish for three days in the same way that Jesus would be in the heart of the earth for three days. The religious leaders were left with a big blank.

Has this been helpful for you? Are you ready to try any of these "Biblical examples" for making decisions in your life?

Let me provide you with one key verse for making good decisions, and the opposite is the main reason people make bad decisions. Here's the verse: "He will give you all you need from day to day if you live for him and make the Kingdom of God your primary concern." Matthew 6:33 (NLT). You may be more familiar with it being stated, "Seek ye first the kingdom of God, and his righteousness; and all these things shall be added unto you." Matthew 6:33 (KJV)

That's it. When you want to make a good decision, ask yourself, "How can I make a decision that will do the most for God in this situation?" and then do it!

Here's the opposite (the key to making bad decisions): ask yourself, "How can I make a decision that will do the most for ME in this situation?" and then do it! The root of bad decisions is ego (sometimes called "Me, Myself, and I").

In case you didn't catch it, let me give it to you again, from another verse. "If you try to keep your life for yourself, you will lose it. But if you give up your life for me, you will find true life." Matthew 16:25 (NLT)

I should warn you that the majority of the people in this world are out for themselves, so they will give you all sorts of strategies to make decisions, like considering the consequences, weighing all options, getting advice from others, looking at your own goals, and even praying about it. But the final decision they recommend is to do what you think is best (for you).

And I'm telling you to make every decision based on what you think would be best for God. Do everything you can for Him, and let Him do everything He will for you!

What About Being Blessed?

"BLESS THE

LORD, O MY

SOUL, AND ALL

THAT IS WITHIN

ME, BLESS HIS

HOLY NAME."

Question: *What does it mean to be "blessed"?*

Answer: *It's good, very good!*

I've heard some form of the word "bless" in a number of settings, such as:

- "Bless you" (after sneezing).

- "God bless you" (a form of "thank you," such as after you give a homeless person some food).

- "I feel really blessed" (I have it good).

- "It was such a blessing to be here" (I liked this!).

- "Bless me, my father, bless me" (Esau, feeling left out of getting the birthright for the firstborn).

- "Bless the Lord, O my soul, and all that is within me, bless His holy name" (a Psalm of David's).

- "May the Lord be gracious unto you and bless you" (a benediction).

- "You'll be blessed" (Elton John lyrics).

- Bless the Beasts and Children (title of a book and a play, also a 1970s song by Karen Carpenter offering something for the underdogs or the weak in comparison to the strong).

- God bless America (I have strong feelings of patriotism and spirituality mixed together).

- "Bless this house, O Lord, we pray" (lyrics from an Irish blessing song and prayer that we sang at the dedication of our new house when we moved in).

- "I'm sure God will bless you" (you'll get a great payback from God).

Where have you heard someone mention something about "blessing"? When do you use it?

According to the dictionary, the word "blessed" comes from the old English word "blood," and it's used in consecration. It could mean to hallow or consecrate by religious rite or word, to hallow with the sign of the cross, to invoke divine care (bless your heart), to praise or glorify (bless His holy name), to speak well of, to confer prosperity or happiness upon, protect, preserve, endow, favor (blessed with athletic ability).

The meaning of "blessed" goes back to the Old Testament Hebrew words *barak* and *ashre* that get translated "bless." The New Testament Greek words *eulogeo* and *markarios* also get translated as "bless." Here are some examples that I found in *The Seventh-day Adventist Bible Commentary.*

God's blessing happens when God gives good gifts to someone (see 2 Samuel 6:11, 12; Job 42:12).

When people "bless" God, they are simply acknowledging God as the one who gives spiritual and material prosperity (see Psalm 63:4; 103:1-5; 145:2).

When one person blesses another, that person is expressing a wish that the other one will be given good gifts (see Joshua 14:13; 1 Samuel 2:20).

Blessed can mean happy or fortunate (see Psalm 1:1; 2:12; 32:1, 2; Matthew 5:1-12).

If every good gift has its origins in God (see James 1:17), then every blessing has its origins in God as well. But the blessings we receive from God aren't merely for us. We are blessed in order to bless others, which has been God's intention from the beginning (see Genesis 1:28-31). He repeated it when He promised a blessing to Abram—a blessing that would reach everyone on earth through Abram (see Genesis12:2, 3).

The same is true today. Every blessing that God gives us is for our benefit and for us to share with others. So bless you! Oh, God has already done that? Well, He's doing it some more. Enjoy it, and pass it along by blessing others, too!

Every blessing that God gives us is for our benefit and for us to share with others.

What About Being Called a Christian?

PETER INTERPRETS HIS DREAM TO MEAN THAT THE GENTILES— PEOPLE THE JEWS FORMERLY CONSIDERED "UNCLEAN"— WERE ALSO CALLED TO BE FOLLOWERS OF JESUS.

Question: *Since Jesus was a Jew, why are His followers called Christians and not Jews?*

Answer: *Jesus was also a male, so why aren't His followers called males? If Jesus were Latino, should His followers be called Latinos?*

Jews trace their background to the Israelites, all the way back to Abraham. You can read about Jewish origin in Genesis 12:1-3. God's call to Abram (later called Abraham) included leaving his original community and moving to a new land where God promised to make a great nation from him.

What makes the origin of this great nation supernatural was the fact that Abram and his wife

216

had no children, and that they were well past their child-bearing years. The birth of a nation requires the birth of at least one person. The promised offspring came as a miracle and demonstrated that God's promise was true (see Galatians 4:22, 23).

It was no surprise that the ethnic group through whom God would bless all nations would also be the Messiah's birth line. Jesus came through the birth line of Abraham, the father of the Jewish nation, and through David, the poster king for the Jews (see Matthew 1:1).

When people killed Jesus, they used the Roman form of death by torture—crucifixion—since Rome ruled Jerusalem at that time. But the Jewish mob outside Pilate's judgment hall willingly took credit for Jesus' death (see Matthew 27:24-26). This is not a put-down of Jews, but it certainly wouldn't be appropriate to call such people "followers of Jesus."

Just before Jesus returned to heaven, He instructed His disciples to be witnesses where Jews lived, but then to go to the entire world (see Acts 1:8). Some may have thought Jesus meant that they should go witness only to Jews throughout the world, since what happened with the miracle of speaking different languages snatched the attention of so many Jews visiting Jerusalem on the day of Pentecost (see Acts 2).

Reading on, Acts 10 contains a story about a strange dream of "unclean" animals that God instructed Peter to eat. Such action was unthinkable for Jews. But in Acts 11, Peter interprets his dream to mean that the Gentiles—people the Jews formerly considered "unclean"—were also called to be followers of Jesus (Acts 11:18).

This opened the floodgates for the news of Jesus, the Christ (Christ means "Messiah" or "Promised One"), to people of all ethnic groups, who became followers of Jesus. As the word spread north to Antioch, the followers of Jesus in Jerusalem sent Barnabas to Antioch. That's where Saul joined Barnabas for a year, and together they taught people about Jesus Christ. According to Acts 11:26, "The disciples were called Christians first at Antioch." And the name seems to have stuck.

If you're a follower of Christ, you're a Christian. By the way, you're also a spiritual child of Abraham, too, because the promises that God gave to Abraham are for all followers of Jesus.

What About Why Bad Things Happen?

PEOPLE WILL CONTINUE TO DEFY GOD UNTIL THE END OF THIS WORLD. AND SATAN IS THE ONE WHO DESERVES THE CREDIT FOR ALL DEFIANCE AND WICKEDNESS ON THIS PLANET, WHICH WILL CONTINUE AND EVEN APPEAR TO BE WINNING UNTIL IT ENDS IN THE LAKE OF FIRE.

(REVELATION 20:10-15)

Question: *Is it because we defy God's Word that so many wicked things are happening?*

Answer: *It's not so much that we defy God's Word—it's because we defy God.*

Those who defy God will eventually regret it. God is the source of life (Genesis 2:7), so defying Him can be deadly. Remember Uzzah's story in 2 Samuel 6:7? Usually, though, God doesn't strike sinners dead, since He isn't "wanting anyone to perish, but everyone to come to repentance" (2 Peter 3:9).

Even before Moses started writing God's Word, an Egyptian Pharaoh oppressed God's people. And eventually God sent Moses to deliver them. But Pharaoh defied God (see Exodus 5-10).

218

And after Pharaoh defied God, God sent a plague. Pharaoh asked for a reprieve, and God gave it, followed by a request to release the Israelites. This cycle repeated itself 10 times. Not until Pharaoh's son was killed did he finally let the Israelites go. But then he chased them and ended up dying (Exodus 14).

God's Word is full of stories about people and how they related to God. For something new, read Amos 3 and 4 to hear God's warning to the people of Israel who consistently defied Him. This defiance continued in the time of Jesus (John 8) and culminated at His death, which He predicted (Matthew 21:33-46).

It sounds simple—sit on the stove and you get burned; defy God and wicked things happen. But it's not always that simple. Remember, the devil's wreaking havoc on this earth, making God look like the bad guy, until you finally figure it out.

Revelation 12:9 reminds us, "The great dragon was hurled down—that ancient serpent called the devil, or Satan, who leads the whole world astray. He was hurled to the earth, and his angels with him."

No wonder a guy like Job, who hadn't done anything wrong at all, suffered things that made it seem as if he'd been bad (getting burned for sitting on the stove). In fact, all the bad things happened to Job because God was so sure Job would trust Him no matter what wickedness came to him (see Job 1).

People will continue to defy God until the end of this world. And Satan is the one who deserves the credit for all defiance and wickedness on this planet, which will continue and even appear to be winning until it ends in the lake of fire (Revelation 20:10-15).

Then God's Word promises, "I heard a loud voice from the throne saying, 'Now the dwelling of God is with men, and he will live with them. They will be his people, and God himself will be with them and be their God. He will wipe every tear from their eyes. There will be no more death or mourning or crying or pain, for the old order of things has passed away'" Revelation 21:3, 4.

I am so looking forward to that time. Aren't you?

What About Anger— Is It a Sin?

"BE YE ANGRY,
AND SIN NOT: LET
NOT THE SUN GO
DOWN UPON
YOUR WRATH."

(EPHESIANS 4:26)

Question: *Is anger a sin?*

Answer: *It might surprise you to know that many people think anger is a sin—a really bad sin. But then it might surprise you to know that many people think anger is not a sin.*

O ne of the most common verses people turn to for an answer to your question is Ephesians 4:26. The King James Version says, "Be ye angry, and sin not: let not the sun go down upon your wrath."

Now, the *King James Version* can sometimes be confusing, since most of us don't use that style of language anymore. But the verse seems to be telling us to be angry and also not to sin. Is that possible?

Here's the same verse from the *New Living Translation*: "And don't sin by letting anger gain control over you. Don't let the sun go down while you are still angry." Verse 27 adds, "For anger gives a mighty foothold to the Devil."

That seems fairly clear to me. Anger isn't sin. Often people do destructive things because of their anger, which makes anger seem like the problem. Yet anger is simply an emotion that indicates how we feel about something.

Let me illustrate my point. If one of your friends started spreading bad rumors about you and you heard about it, there's a good chance you'd feel angry. Is that a sin?

No. Your anger would probably stem from your hurt and surprise that your friend would do something like that. Some people might simply cry about it, while others would probably move into anger mode.

How you respond to your friend's actions is where sin comes into play. For instance, if you decide to spread rumors about your friend because you're angry that he or she did that to you, it's certainly not a godly response.

Paul quotes Proverbs 25:21, 22 when he writes about being good and kind—even to your enemies. He says it's like heaping coals of fire onto their heads. Then he gives his own comment: "Don't let evil get the best of you, but conquer evil by doing good" (Romans 12:21, NLT).

So if you're feeling angry, ask yourself where this feeling stems from. Then, instead of responding with something to hurt others (because they hurt you), give them a little taste of heaven, not hell!

Oh, and by the way, get a concordance and look up the word "anger." You'll find that Jesus felt anger (Mark 3:5). The Psalms often talk about God's anger (Psalm 78:58), and one Psalm even requests that God get angry (Psalm 69:24). Isaiah and Jeremiah write about it frequently, too.

Is anger a sin? No. It's an indicator that something really matters to you. How you respond to what caused your anger is your opportunity to showcase either good or evil.

What About Killing When You're in the Military?

"DO NOT BE AFRAID OF THOSE WHO KILL THE BODY BUT CANNOT KILL THE SOUL. RATHER, BE AFRAID OF THE ONE WHO CAN DESTROY BOTH SOUL AND BODY IN HELL."

(MATTHEW 10:28)

Question: *I've enlisted in the military, and I'm about to go to boot camp. Someday I might end up on the front lines and have to kill somebody. I know the Ten Commandments say, "Thou shalt not kill" (Exodus 20:13, KJV). But the Bible also has stories about battles where lots of people were killed. Will God look down on me if I have to kill someone?*

Answer: *You're right! The Bible does say not to kill people, and then it describes lots of killing. That sounds like a direct contradiction, doesn't it?*

The sixth commandment reads "Thou shalt not kill" (Exodus 20:13, KJV). Most *translations (even the New King James Version) render it, "You shall not murder."*

You see, there are seven different Hebrew words in the Old Testament for our English word "kill." The one used in the Ten Commandments—*ratsach*—refers to premeditated killing, or what we'd refer to as first-degree murder. An example would be getting so angry at somebody that you plot a way to kill that person, and then you carry it out.

Some Bible scholars have pointed out that this type of killing doesn't refer to killing animals (Genesis 9:3), defending one's home from nighttime burglars (Exodus 22:2), accidental killings (Deuteronomy 19:5), execution by the government (capital punishment) of those who've committed murder (Genesis 9:6), or involvement in certain types of war—similar to what you refer to when Israel went to war (Numbers 31:17; Joshua 6:21).

Other people simply don't buy that. Because humans have been made in the very image of God (Genesis 1:27), killing a person is seen as a form of attack against God Himself. In fact, some people are pacifists to the point that they oppose the death of not just humans but animals as well. These people would probably see the above explanation as somebody just trying to weasel out an answer to support the bias they have towards killing in the first place.

Interestingly, in Genesis 9:6 God told Noah after the flood that whoever kills a person must be killed. The reason God gave for this law was that He'd made humans in His image. Yet God gave this instruction right after the Flood—an event that wiped out everyone not in the ark. Confusing?

People in the military aren't the only professionals who have to wrestle with this issue. Law enforcement personnel deal with it, too. Although police officers don't kill criminals nearly as often as is depicted on TV, there are times they might be faced with killing another human being. Does that mean we shouldn't have a police force? And should we not have a military?

Most people accept the need for a military and a police force. Of course, they want a humane force rather than an aggressive one.

Unfortunately, most of life isn't as simple as outright hostility or peaceful retreat. Things get mixed up–whether it's bombing a country because they're increasing their military might, or shooting a man of a different race when he reaches for his wallet ("I thought he was going to pull a gun"), or invading a foreign country to protect our financial interests.

Yet God is for life. Jesus said, "The thief comes only to steal and kill and destroy; I have come that they may have life, and have it to the full" (John 10:10).

Jesus also said, "Do not be afraid of those who kill the body but cannot kill the soul. Rather, be afraid of the One who can destroy both soul and body in hell" (Matthew 10:28). Each person must face death—both death on this planet and the possibility of an eternal death (or eternal life). Both count.

But strangely, in promoting life sometimes you must kill. If a crazy man goes on a shooting spree, it might require shooting him so that he won't kill any more people. In a war, killing people is done to put an end to the war. Indeed, killing to save life can be very strange.

If you go into the military, you'll be trained to kill and to do it efficiently. You will take orders from a superior officer rather than making those kinds of decisions for yourself. A military doesn't work if each person decides for himself or herself what to do. You must obey orders.

I applaud you for asking yourself these hard questions that don't have nice and easy answers. Just remember that God is for life. And I'd be interested to hear from you how you are trained to respect and promote life. That's what I'd want my military and police force to do. How about you?

What About Masturbation?

WHEN A PERSON MASTURBATES, THEY COULD BE HAVING A FANTASY ABOUT HAVING SEX WITH SOMEONE THAT THEY DON'T PERSONALLY KNOW—A MOVIE STAR, A MUSIC STAR, A FRIEND, ANYONE.

Question: *Does the bible say anything about whether or not masturbation is wrong?*

Answer: *The Bible mentions many behaviors, but masturbation is not one of them. You won't find the word in the Bible, or anything like it. Masturbation is "the M word" that most people don't talk about. Since masturbation is a private activity, most people keep it private.*

In case there happens to be someone reading this who isn't sure what masturbation is, let me provide a technical definition from the online Merriam-Webster's Dictionary: "Erotic stimulation especially of one's own genital organs commonly resulting in orgasm and achieved by manual or other bodily contact exclusive of sexual intercourse, by instrumental manipulation, occasionally by sexual fantasies, or by various combinations of these agencies."

You ask, "Is it wrong?" Since the Bible doesn't mention masturbation, some figure they can just come up with their own moral decision apart from any word from God. Others take the opposite approach and think that if God didn't mention it, then it must not matter to Him.

I've found that outspoken voices beyond the Christian community answer sexual questions on a "choose-whatever-you-want" basis. Sometimes they add the condition "choose whatever you want as long as it doesn't hurt anybody else." I can't agree with that. Unlike animals in heat driven to mate, God created human beings for a highly sensual experience through sexual intercourse. He wired our brains so that this expression would be far more than merely sex. For humans, this act is supposed to be based on the intimacy between two people who are married to each other.

When a person masturbates, they could be having a fantasy about having sex with someone that they don't personally know—a movie star, a music star, a friend, anyone. This approach to sexuality is certainly self-centered rather than selfless—the way God designed sexual expression to be.

The immediate gratification element associated with masturbation can create problems later when a person is traveling the winding pathway of a relationship with a real person. For most people, their sex drive begins during their early adolescent years. In Bible times this is the age when people got married. But in the Western world today, marriage doesn't come for more than a decade after adolescence for many people.

The Bible does have a few things to say about that. First Thessalonians 4:3-8 provides helpful guidance. In *The Living Bible* it reads: "For God wants you to be holy and pure, and to keep clear of all sexual sin so that each of you will marry in holiness and honor—not in lustful passion as the heathen do, in their ignorance of God and his ways. And this also is God's will: that you never cheat in this matter by taking another man's wife, because the Lord will punish you terribly for this, as we have solemnly told you before. For God has not called us to be dirty-minded and full of lust, but to be holy and clean. If anyone refuses to live by these rules he is not disobeying the rules of men but of God who gives his Holy Spirit to you." That's clear, isn't it? Also, I recommend that you read 1 Corinthians 6:13-20 in *The Living Bible*.

God created us as sexual beings, but our sexuality is something that needs direction, restraint, expression, and focus. If you think that getting married will solve your sexual expression binge, guess again. Your sexuality is something for you to live with the rest of your life, including old age—if you live that long. So living as a Christian with your God-given sexuality is something you need to do not only during your adolescent years but for all of your remaining years.

Let's return to your question: Does the Bible say anything about whether or not masturbation is wrong? No. However, it does point out that God's gift of sex is often misused by the world, and that God desires for us to be pure. Above all, He always desires the best for us—no substitutes.

> So living as a Christian with your God-given sexuality is something you need to do not only during your adolescent years but for all of your remaining years.

What About My Mind Wandering When I Pray?

MANY PEOPLE FIND IT CHALLENGING TO KEEP THEIR PRAYER LIFE ON TRACK. SO YOU'RE NOT ALONE.

Question: *When I pray, sometimes I find that my mind isn't totally focused on God or holy things. For example, my mind may wander off and replay a song that I just listened to, or I may think about something I need to do after I finish praying. Am I doing something wrong? Is my prayer not acceptable to God?*

Answer: *Many people find it challenging to keep their prayer life on track. So you're not alone.*

Y*our mind could be wandering for a variety of reasons. Maybe you're thinking of 12 to 14 other things while you're trying to pray. Maybe you're feeling* *rushed— "I have only 18 seconds to pray right now." Or maybe you don't have much to say to God: "And bless the missionaries and colporteurs across the seas—again."*

I've found that setting aside some time to pray really helps. If you aren't accustomed to praying, set aside two to five minutes, but carve out 10-15 minutes in case your conversation starts to focus and flow.

Some people write down their prayers in a prayer journal. Others sit quietly and wait until the chaos in their head slows down. I've discovered that praying with my eyes open helps me focus better than praying with them closed.

You mentioned that your mind sometimes replays a song you were just listening to. Why not lead into your prayer time by listening to a song that would direct your mind to God? Or read a passage of Scripture and then pray your way through it, using it as an outline for your prayer. Are you one of those people who likes lists? Perhaps a prayer list could give your prayer time structure and progression.

If you're praying in a sort of free-form way, you can expect your mind to wander. But use that wandering as part of your prayer. For example, you might be praying about a test in algebra that's causing you anxiety. Then your mind jumps to Cathy, who always does so well on tests. Then thinking of Cathy reminds you of that funny-faced person you saw on TV the other night. Your mind then jumps to why you're a night person and so are your friends. Then you wonder what in the world you were praying about in the first place.

If your mind is jumping around like that, pray about the algebra test. Pray for Cathy and celebrate her success, and ask God to remove your jealousy about her high scores. And when you think about that funny-faced person on TV, thank God for His sense of humor, and pray that you won't laugh at the expense of other people. And as far as you being a night person, remember that God is the master and owner of the day and the night (see Psalm 74:16). So thank Him for both, and that you don't have to be the master of either. And you've just prayed quite a bit!

A form of prayer I've come to appreciate the past few years is praying through the Psalms. I didn't write them, but they often express my hopes and desires, my frustrations and fears, my confusion and anger. In fact, sometimes I'll mark a certain psalm for good times or another one for bad times, etc. I've found that *The Message* is a fresh paraphrase that states a psalm more like my guts would say it than like perfect poetry. Here's an example from Psalm 32:1, 2:

"Count yourself lucky, how happy you must be—you get a fresh start, your slate's wiped clean.

"Count yourself lucky—God holds nothing against you and you're holding nothing back from him."

As far as whether or not you're praying "right," that's almost like wondering if your conversation with one of your friends went right. The good news is that you can be more open and honest with God than you can be with your closest friend. It's not a matter of some magical formula or chant. Remember, God's already listening. So keep talking!

The good news is that you can be more open and honest with God than you can be with your closest friend. It's not a matter of some magical formula or chant. Remember, God's already listening. So keep talking!

What About Praying for Someone to Like Me?

THE PREACHER
POINTED OUT
THAT INSTEAD OF
HOLDING IT IN OR
SPEWING IT OUT,
THE PLACE TO GO
WITH YOUR
ANGER IS TO
GOD, BECAUSE
GOD CAN HANDLE
IT.

Question: *Is it OK to pray for a person to like you?*

Answer: *By all means—yes! In fact, that's probably the first and best place to start! Note the first five words of your question: "Is it OK to pray?"*

S*ome people might suggest that there are certain things we shouldn't pray for, such as praying for something bad to happen to someone when you're angry with that person. Others would say that praying for something you want for potentially selfish reasons isn't the correct way to pray either.*

When I read Psalms, I find all kinds of prayers that seem to be "incorrect." For example, notice these lines from Psalm 109, with my comments in parentheses:

"Wicked and deceitful men have opened their mouths against me" (verse 2). (I've got some bad dudes out to get me.)

"When he is tried, let him be found guilty, and may his prayers condemn him" (verse 7). (Lord, get him instead of letting him get me, and twist his prayers so they work against him instead of for him!)

"May his children be fatherless and his wife a widow" (verse 9). (Kill him!)

"May his descendants be cut off" (verse 13). (Go ahead and kill his children, too!)

"May the iniquity of his fathers be remembered before the Lord" (verse 14). (Don't get just the family members after him; get the ones before him, too.)

"May a creditor seize all he has" (verse 11). (A total wipeout is needed, including his reputation.)

Read the entire Psalm, and you'll find that it's the prayer of a person who is angry and probably very hurt, too. Is this kind of prayer OK?

My initial reaction is "No, because David isn't being very nice." But I heard a sermon one time titled "I'm So Mad I Could Pray" that changed my mind.

The preacher described how some people hold in their anger and it eats away at them. Others decide to let it out, so they target their anger at the person who made them angry, even though that usually makes things worse.

The preacher pointed out that instead of holding it in or spewing it out, the place to go with your anger is to God, because God can handle it. Now, that's quite a friend to have!

The same is true about other intense feelings, such as wanting a person to like you. God already knows what you'd like, so it's not a matter of exposing a secret. You can trust Him.

I'm guessing that your question is about someone of the opposite sex liking you. I'd certainly make that part of my prayer life if I were you.

But the Bible speaks more about your loving other people than it speaks about other people loving you. Check this out: "Love one another. As I have loved you, so you must love one another. By this all men will know that you are my disciples, if you love one another" (John 13:34, 35).

"You have heard that it was said, 'Love your neighbor and hate your enemy.' But I tell you: Love your enemies and pray for those who persecute you" (Matthew 5:43, 44).

Yes, I think it's fine to pray that another person will like you. But then trust God with the results.

You must realize that God isn't a magical genie who merely grants wishes and then disappears. God likes you, but just because you ask Him to help someone like you doesn't mean He will manipulate that person into doing it.

God is more interested in your becoming someone likable than He is in getting somebody to like you. So pray for that special someone to like you, and then be open for God to change you into a person like Him.

"You have heard that it was said, 'Love your neighbor and hate your enemy.' But I tell you: Love your enemies and pray for those who persecute you."

(Matthew 5:43, 44)

What About Getting Myself Organized?

"WHY BE LIKE THE PAGANS WHO ARE SO DEEPLY CONCERNED ABOUT THESE THINGS? YOUR HEAVENLY FATHER ALREADY KNOWS ALL YOUR NEEDS, AND HE WILL GIVE YOU ALL YOU NEED FROM DAY TO DAY IF YOU LIVE FOR HIM AND MAKE THE KINGDOM OF GOD YOUR PRIMARY CONCERN."

(MATTHEW 6:32, 33, NLT)

Question: *I'm a college student who's so preoccupied with my studies that I don't have time to witness to a friend, conduct a Bible study, or help the needy—unless I do it on Sabbath. What's the best way to organize myself so I can do these things for God?*

Answer: *Organizing yourself is an issue of self-discipline that involves choices and consequences. Everyone has 24 hours a day, but that's about where the similarity stops. Some need more sleep than others. Some have to work more hours than others. Some students need to study more than others, etc.*

Take some time to identify your long-term goals, such as what you'd like to do after college. Then look at how your short-term goals contribute to your long-term goals. You can go a step further and organize your goals for this school year, even this semester.

As you're identifying your goals, seek counsel from people you respect. Beware, some will tell you about how to make money or how to become famous. And some will focus on selecting a spouse, or getting a job within the Seventh-day Adventist Church.

Perhaps the most important passage of Scripture I can share with you is God's promise to care for you when you place Him as your first priority. "Why be like the pagans who are so deeply concerned about these things? Your heavenly Father already knows all your needs, and he will give you all you need from day to day if you live for him and make the Kingdom of God your primary concern" (Matthew 6:32, 33, NLT).

Here are my recommendations. Commit yourself anew to Jesus. Do your very best in what you're currently doing—going to college. And watch for indications of God's activity that you can acknowledge and for which you can give Him praise.

You mentioned that you have time to help others only on Sabbath. For years Adventists have seen Sabbath as a time to worship God in church and in scheduled faith-sharing activities. Jesus pointed out that Sabbath is a day for doing good, for helping others (see Matthew 12:12). Of course, every day is a good day to help others, but especially on Sabbath!

It sounds as if you've heard people say you need to witness to a friend, conduct a Bible study, or help the needy. Have you considered the possibility that these things can happen right in your current situation?

Witnessing to a friend isn't something you do from 3:30 to 4:15 p.m. on Tuesdays. It's what you do all the time. Instead of conducting a Bible study, why not join one and actively participate in it? How about studying with a fellow classmate? You could pray with fellow students or ask a student or teacher to pray for you—on the spot.

Live for Jesus in your daily life as you take classes to prepare you for greater service. If you aren't serving others now, you probably won't serve anyone but yourself when you graduate either. But if you develop the attitude and actions of serving others now, you'll do the same later, too. It's all a matter of priorities!

But if you develop the attitude and actions of serving others now, you'll do the same later, too. It's all a matter of priorities!

What About Academics at an Adventist School?

Question: *Should I go to a Seventh-day Adventist school even if their academic program isn't good?*

Answer: *It all depends on how smart you are!*

Some people who do well academically want bigger challenges than a relatively small school can usually provide; they want advanced classes. Others who do poorly academically want remedial classes, which bigger schools are more likely to provide.

But there are some educators who prefer to put all students together in one group to "mainstream" them, rather than separate "smart" people from "dumb" people. They've found that these labels aren't very helpful most of the time.

Hopefully you're smart enough to know that there's more to school than just academics. Some people think academics are the most important thing to consider when selecting a school. I certainly don't. Of course academics are part of the picture, but I wouldn't rate it as my first priority. My primary interest is in character development. So that's the question I'd ask first when it comes to choosing a school.

Allow me to rephrase your question: Should I go to a Seventh-day Adventist (SDA) school even if their character development program isn't good? My answer would be no! But then I'd want to know more about why you think the SDA school isn't strong on character development. Most of the ones I've been in contact with give it top priority.

Your question reminds me of the worldly priority of selfishness that takes the form of getting the best for one's self so you can climb higher, achieve the most, and get more than anybody else. Christ's disciples had this attitude, and here's how He responded to them:

"You know that in this world kings are tyrants, and officials lord it over the people beneath them. But among you it should be quite different. Whoever wants to be a leader among you must be your servant, and whoever wants to be first must become your slave. For even I, the Son of Man, came here not to be served but to serve others, and to give my life as a ransom for many" (Matthew 20:25-28, NLT).

Another way of saying it is, "Seek ye first the kingdom of God, and His righteousness; and all these things shall be added unto you" (Matthew 6:33, KJV). A paraphrase of that verse says, "So don't worry at all about having enough food and clothing. Why be like the heathen? For they take pride in all these things and are deeply concerned about them. But your heavenly Father already knows perfectly well that you need them, and he will give them to you if you give him first place in your life and live as he wants you to" (Matthew 6:31-33, TLB).

So when it comes to selecting a school, choose one that puts God ahead of academics, and the academics will take care of themselves. It's important to realize that putting God first doesn't result in poor academics. By putting academics in their proper place, you can actually do better academically than you would otherwise. If I were you, I'd be concerned about an SDA school that put academics first, because that's not a smart thing to do based on God's counsel.

And academically, students who go to SDA schools score higher, as a group, than those who go to public school. Their SAT scores are higher, their GPAs are higher, and the more years a student attends an Adventist school, the better the student does academically. Adventist academics are actually quite high. But that's what you would expect when a school puts God first.

Excellence comes from God, not from one's self, even though it takes all you've got as well. But the purpose of excellence is service, not selfishness. So choose a school that puts God first and deals with you as a whole person, not just your mind.

Excellence comes from God, not from one's self, even though it takes all you've got as well. But the purpose of excellence is service, not selfishness. So choose a school that puts God first and deals with you as a whole person, not just your mind.

What About Pets Going to Heaven?

JESUS DID SAY THAT PEOPLE WERE MORE IMPORTANT THAN ANIMALS (SEE MATTHEW 12:11, 12), WHICH DOESN'T MEAN THAT ANIMALS DON'T COUNT. IT'S JUST THAT HUMANS ARE MORE IMPORTANT.

Question: *My cat died recently, and I want to know if she'll be in heaven. I've heard "No, she won't be there," and I've heard "Yes, she will be there." I'm confused. Do you know the answer?*

Answer: *Anyone who's been close to a pet wants to be assured that their pet will be with them in heaven. But the Bible doesn't give a clear yes or no on the topic. So that's probably why you've heard both answers.*

As you mature you'll discover that there are plenty of other topics the Bible doesn't come right out and say yes or no about. So for those looking to the Bible as an answer book, this can be disappointing. But the Bible isn't intended to be a dictionary or encyclopedia.

It seems to me that the Bible was written as a communication tool for God to be in contact with humans and for humans to understand God better. Perhaps we can find out enough about God to come up with an idea of whether or not our pets will be in heaven.

Since God is love (1 John 4:8), and since heaven is a wonderful place God is preparing for His people (John 14:1-3), surely God would include a special pet as part of heaven. After all, God created all the animals in the first place, actually forming them out of the dust of the earth (see Genesis 2:19), just as He did Adam (Genesis 2:7).

Because God commanded Adam and Eve to be masters over the rest of creation (Genesis 1:28), many people make a clear separation between humans and other parts of God's creation.

And although the rest of creation suffered from Adam and Eve's rebellion against God and suffered a similar fate during the Flood, God spared a portion of the animals in the ark, enough to keep those species alive. In that sense God did "save" the animals, at least during the Flood.

When Jesus came to save humanity, He demonstrated even more tenderness and compassion than most people expected (Matthew 5:38-48). He included women and children, who were often excluded by others (Luke 7:36-8:3; Mark 10:13-16).

But I'm not aware of any examples in the Gospels that describe Jesus healing an animal or resurrecting a pet or farm animal. I'm not saying that it didn't happen. I'm just saying that if it did happen, it wasn't recorded in the Bible.

Jesus did say that people were more important than animals (see Matthew 12:11, 12), which doesn't mean that animals don't count. It's just that humans are more important.

Will your pet be in heaven? I don't know. But I do know that all of creation is looking forward to the end of this earth. Perhaps if we look forward to it as well, that hope will sustain us while we wait to see Jesus and all He has in store for us in heaven!

More Questions About Life

- ◆ PEER PRESSURE?
- ◆ PIERCINGS, TATTOOS, AND JEWELRY?
- ◆ TALKING TO UNBELIEVERS?
- ◆ AN UNWANTED PREGNANCY?
- ◆ ABORTION?
- ◆ DANCING—IS IT WRONG?
- ◆ MAKEUP?
- ◆ GRADUATIONS ON SABBATH?
- ◆ COMPETING ON SABBATH?
- ◆ CUSSING?
- ◆ GETTING MONEY FOR A MISSION TRIP?

What About Peer Pressure?

Question: *My friends are always pressuring me to do things with them that I know are wrong, like drinking alcohol. I go along with them because they help me out a lot financially, so I feel as if I shouldn't just "diss" them. But what should I do?*

Answer: *From a distance the answer is easy—drop those friends and find some new ones. They aren't really your friends if they're pressuring you to do things you know are wrong.*

Now, *if that's all you needed to hear, stop reading the rest of this response. But if that isn't enough of an answer, continue reading.*

Everyone wants friends. Are you a good friend?

Here are a few questions for your friendship barometer: Are you the kind of person others want to be around? Are you a good listener? Can you carry on a conversation? What types of things do you do for fun? Do you care about others, or are you more concerned about yourself? Do you build people up rather than tear them down? Are you more concerned about what others think, or about what's right?

Here's what Solomon said about having friends, "There are 'friends' who destroy each other, but a real friend sticks closer than a brother" (Proverbs 18:24, NLT).

Many people have found God to be their best friend, and sometimes their only friend. God's promise is "I will never leave you or forsake you" (promised to Joshua who was a little nervous; see Deuteronomy 31:6, 8; quoted in Hebrews 13:5).

When you are confident that God is always there for you, you won't be swayed by what others might do to you or pressure you to do (see Hebrews 13:6).

I have one more suggestion for you. People often talk about giving in to peer pressure at all ages. Sometimes all you need is for one person to stand up with you. If you're feeling especially weak or vulnerable, maybe that person needs to be the first to stand, and then you can join that person.

It sounds as though you need to find that person. Ask your pastor or some other church leader you respect to hook you up with someone who can stand with you when you need some support.

Here's how Solomon put it in Ecclesiastes 4:9-12: "Two people can accomplish more than twice as much as one; they get a better return for their labor. If one person falls, the other can reach out and help. But people who are alone when they fall are in real trouble. And on a cold night, two under the same blanket can gain warmth from each other. But how can one be warm alone? A person standing alone can be attacked and defeated, but two can stand back-to-back and conquer. Three are even better, for a triple-braided cord is not easily broken" (NLT).

I'd say it's time to get anchored into God and find the kind of friend you'd really like. Then you can be a positive influence on others instead of being influenced by others to do things you don't really want to do.

What About Piercings, Tattoos, and Jewelry?

"YOU SHALL NOT MAKE ANY CUTTINGS IN YOUR FLESH FOR THE DEAD, NOR TATTOO ANY MARKS ON YOU: I AM THE LORD."

LEVITICUS 19:28

Question: *Does the Bible have anything to say about piercings, tattoos, and jewelry?*

Answer: *Yes, the Bible does have a few things to say about piercings, tattoos, and jewelry. We'll start with piercings, and then we'll integrate tattoos and include jewelry.*

L*et's start with Jesus! You may have seen the T-shirt or bumper sticker that says, "Body piercing saved my life." It's followed by artwork of a hand and wrist nailed to a cross.*

In John 19:34 you can read, "One of the soldiers pierced Jesus' side with a spear, bringing a sudden flow of blood and water." And then a few verses later it says, "These things happened so that the scripture would be fulfilled: 'Not one of his bones will be broken,' and, as another scripture says, 'They will look on the one they have pierced'" (36, 37). The first scripture referred to is Psalm 34:20, and the second one—the one about being pierced—refers to Zechariah 12:10.

By the way, the ones who pierced Jesus—all who actively participated in His crucifixion—will see Him coming in power and glory (see Revelation 1:7). I expect to be elated to see Jesus, don't you? But those who pierced Him 2,000 years ago, and those in every nation who are figuratively killing Him again (see Hebrews 6:6), will not be so happy to see the One they've pierced.

I don't think my response so far is answering the question intended when you asked about piercings, but this is the primary piercing that the Bible talks about.

When Mary, Jesus' mother, presented Him in the Temple as a baby, Simeon told Mary that one day "a sword will pierce your own soul" because of Jesus (see Luke 2:35). This wasn't a physical piercing, but a piercing of the soul, which can be far more painful than a physical piercing.

Sometimes people do physical piercings as an expression of inner pain. And some people feel inner pain when someone they care about gets a body part pierced! But what does the Bible say about getting your body pierced for cosmetic reasons, like getting your ears or some other body part pierced?

The text most often used against piercings, cutting one's self and getting tattoos is Leviticus 19:28. In the *New King James Version* it reads, "You shall not make any cuttings in your flesh for the dead, nor tattoo any marks on you: I am the Lord."

That's all some people need to know in order to refrain from piercings or tattoos. Others would like it repeated a few times in other places in the Bible, or just not in the context of Leviticus 19.

Leviticus 19:27, the verse right before it, says not to cut the hair on the sides of your head or clip off the edges of your beard. Most people don't make a big deal out of that today, since they figure that was a cultural issue when it was written. It was, and it doesn't apply to our culture today.

But Leviticus 19:29, the verse right after it, says not to degrade your daughter by making her a prostitute, and we certainly wouldn't say that verse is just cultural for that time and doesn't apply today! Making a daughter a prostitute is a very bad thing at any time in any culture!

So, is Leviticus 19:28 saying something only for that culture, or does it apply to us today in our culture?

Leviticus 19:28 gives a clue. Notice the reason it gives for cutting—for the dead. The *New Living Translation* reads, "Never cut your bodies in mourning for the dead or mark your skin with tattoos, for I am the Lord." Another rendering of the verse talks about cutting one's self as part of a funeral rite. I'm not very clear about what was done at that time at funerals. This cutting probably has more to do with self-mutilation, either as a release of personal pain, or a human attempt to try to get the attention or earn the favor of some unpredictable supernatural powers. Remember the story in 1 Kings 18 about the prophets of Baal doing a similar thing on Mount Carmel in an attempt to get Baal's attention (see 1 Kings 18:28)?

The other day, when I picked up some pizzas for our youth group meeting, the person at the cash register had several ear piercings with jewelry, plus various piercings on her face with metal attached to the holes. She had difficulty talking to me because her tongue was pierced, and another piece of metal kept the hole from naturally closing up.

I felt pity for her. I wondered why she was going to all that trouble to be cool or to fit in, or what got into her mind to make her think it was a good idea for her to do this to herself. But I realized that my opinion of her didn't matter to her at all. She had done this for other reasons than to get the approval of a middle-aged man.

My mind went to Romans 12:2 in the *New Living Translation*, which reads, "Don't copy the behavior and customs of this world, but let God transform you into a new person by changing the way you think. Then you will know what God wants you to do, and you will know how good and pleasing and perfect his will really is."

I place piercings, tattoos, and jewelry into the category of the behavior and customs of this world that followers of Jesus don't need to follow. But others would put things I've done, like buying an expensive sound system, having a hairstyle I think is cool, trying to accumulate more and more for myself instead of giving things away to others, going to church so others think I'm a good person, etc., into the category of copying the behavior and customs of this world. And they would be right.

But this doesn't mean that you can or should get piercings, just because I'm guilty in copying the world. Instead, both of us would be far better off to let God transform us into new people by changing the way we think! Are you open to that? I am. Are you also willing to talk openly with those who are concerned with you about piercings, tattoos, and jewelry; pray together out loud about it; and truly ask God to transform you—all of you?

Tattoos are pretty much in the same category as piercings—we found them in the same verse in Leviticus. These days tattoos are seen as something negative by some and positive by others. From a practical standpoint, they are more permanent than something printed on a T-shirt, which, I suppose, is the point. But I'm amazed at how little thought some people give to the tattoos that they get. Sometimes I just want to hug them and tell them that God loves them, and that they don't need to go to those extremes to be noticed, accepted, admired, or to "fit in." But then I'm reminded that they usually aren't trying to get me to notice, accept, or admire them, nor are they trying to "fit in" to my world.

Several months ago I read about a bicycle racer (no, not Lance Armstrong) who was denied joining a team because he had so many tattoos. There simply was a rule on that team that you couldn't have tattoos. It wasn't based on anything religious; it was just the rule for that bicycle racing team. So he had to decide which was more important to him—joining the bicycle racing team, or going through the long, painful, and expensive process of having all his tattoos removed. The last I heard, he opted to keep his tattoos and not join the team.

I mention this simply to point out that sometimes the questions we raise in the spiritual realm are dealt with by people outside of the spiritual realm for reasons that have nothing to do with God.

Now, when it comes to jewelry, we can certainly misrepresent God's message when we take a verse out of context and twist it to say something that was never intended. A good example of this is taking part of Ezekiel 16 and using it however you want in an argument about jewelry.

If you want to wear jewelry, just pull out verses 11 to 13, "I gave you lovely jewelry, bracelets, and beautiful necklaces, a ring for your nose and earrings for your ears, and a lovely crown for your head. And so you were made beautiful with gold and silver" (NLT). You can even act as though you're taking this in context by pointing out that God is the one who gives you this jewelry (note verses 18 and 19).

If you are opposed to the wearing of jewelry, focus on portions of verses 37 and 39 to point out that God will "strip you naked in front of them [your enemies] so they can stare at you," and "They [your enemies] will strip you and take your beautiful jewels, leaving you completely naked and ashamed" (NLT).

By the way, jewelry isn't the issue at all in Ezekiel 16. The issue is that God saved His people, entered into a covenant with them, and took care of them, and they broke the covenant and used what God provided for them to follow pagan gods. Amazingly, God still forgives His people (see how Ezekiel 16 ends, verses 59-63). This isn't to give us a green light to wear jewelry or a red light to not wear it; it has to do with being committed to God in all we do, not just symbolically, but in reality.

Why can't you get your body pierced, tattooed, or wear jewelry? Up to some point in your life, others make that decision for you. You will need to listen to them and inquire regarding their reasons for those rules. Sometimes it may be just because they don't want you to do it. Sometimes they haven't thought it through themselves. Sometimes they have reasons, but can't articulate them well. Sometimes you don't listen very well, because you already want to do what you want to do.

I suggest that you come up with the reason(s) that you want to get piercings, tattoos, or wear jewelry. See if your reason(s) have anything to do with God or not. Then pray openly and ask God to bring you conviction.

You need to get your own connection with God going strong, because one day when you're outside of your parents' house, you're going to do what you think is best. If you don't have your connection with God clear at that time, you'll end up doing some pretty stupid things instead of doing God's will for your life. Would God really tell you to get pierced, tattooed, or wear jewelry?

Because of all that God has done for you (see Romans 12:1), live by what God tells you in verse 2: "Don't copy the behavior and customs of this world, but let God transform you into a new person by changing the way you think. Then you will know what God wants you to do, and you will know how good and pleasing and perfect his will really is" (NLT).

You need to get your own connection with God going strong, because one day when you're outside of your parents' house, you're going to do what you think is best.

What About Talking to Unbelievers?

AT OTHER TIMES IT'S BETTER TO LISTEN FIRST AND THEN RESPOND TO WHAT OTHERS SAY, AS WHEN JESUS RESPONDED TO THE RICH YOUNG RULER.

Question: *What topics should I bring up when I'm talking to unbelievers about God?*

Answer: *I wish there were a simple answer to your question, but there isn't. If only I could say, "Talk about salvation," or "The best topic is Christ's death." But people who talk about God vary, and so do unbelievers. And what you might talk about one moment may not be the best topic the next.*

What topics do you usually bring up when talking to unbelievers? Sports? The opposite sex? Hairstyles? Young people often talk about the latest media that's impacted them—TV, video, DVD, music, Internet, MySpace, etc.

When you look at Jesus' example, there's not a one-size-fits-all way He talked with unbelievers. Look up these passages and see what topics or tactics Jesus utilized:

1. The rich young ruler (Luke 18:18-23).

2. The multitude (Matthew 5:1-16).

3. Nicodemus (John 3:1-21).

4. Zacchaeus (Luke 19:1-10).

5. The Pharisees and the man with the shriveled hand (Mark 3:1-6).

6. The woman at the well (John 4:5-42).

7. The demoniac (Mark 5:1-20).

8. The Pharisees (Matthew 23:15-28).

9. The woman who anointed Jesus' feet (Mark 14:3-9).

10. Cleansing the Temple (Matthew 21:10-17).

Something I've noticed in these stories is that Jesus treats each person and each situation in a unique way. I think that means we can't use the same formula all the time. Sometimes it's better for us to take the initiative, as when Jesus talked to the woman at the well (John 4:7). At other times it's better to listen first and then respond to what others say, as when Jesus responded to the rich young ruler (Luke 18:18-23).

I've noticed that sometimes Jesus stayed on the topic (Matthew 22:17-22), but at other times He cut to the core (see John 3:2, 3). He also seemed to go after those who weren't very teachable (see Matthew 23—the whole chapter!). But have you noticed that Jesus often protected those who'd been beaten down by others (see Mark 14:3-9)?

When you take time to listen to others, they're more apt to listen to you; it's called "earning the right to be heard." If you tell others about something they're not ready to listen to, it's like planting good seed in bad soil (Matthew 13:18-23) or throwing precious pearls to pigs (Matthew 7:6).

Ask the Holy Spirit to impress you with what to weave into your conversations with unbelievers. For example, when someone asks you what you do for fun, you can tell them about something you did with your youth group or your church. That brings up the topic of God and religious things without saying, "You should go to church," which actually might be the best response in another situation.

When Jesus sent out His disciples to announce His arrival, He told them, "Don't be naive. Some people will impugn your motives, others will smear your reputation—just because you believe in me. Don't be upset when they haul you before the civil authorities. Without knowing it, they've done you—and me—a favor, given you a platform for preaching the kingdom news! And don't worry about what you'll say or how you'll say it. The right words will be there; the Spirit of your Father will supply the words" (Matthew 10:17-20, *The Message*).

If it's not a time to defend yourself when you've been arrested for your alliance with Jesus, remember the counsel of Peter: "Be ready to speak up and tell anyone who asks why you're living the way you are, and always with the utmost courtesy" (1 Peter 3:15, *The Message*).

"Be ready to speak up and tell anyone who asks why you're living the way you are, and always with the utmost courtesy." (1 Peter 3:15, The Message)

What About an Unwanted Pregnancy?

Question: *I've done something that I thought would come later in life. I'm three months pregnant now, and later I'll have to stop school for a few months.*

I don't know what to think. I've considered getting an abortion, but I just can't do it. I made it, so I'm going to have to raise it.

The Lord gave this to me for a reason, but I just don't know why. Can you give me any Bible passages that can help with this little situation?

Answer: *The first Bible passage I think of is 1 Peter 5:7: "Cast all your anxiety on him [God] because he cares for you." Here's another one: "My God will meet all your needs according to his glorious riches" (Philippians 4:19).*

I *like this one too: "Praise be to the God and Father of our Lord Jesus Christ, the Father of compassion and the God of all comfort, who comforts us in all our troubles, so that we can comfort those in any trouble with the comfort we ourselves have received from God" (2 Corinthians 1:3, 4).*

Now I'd like to respond to some of your statements that led to your request for some Bible passages.

It sounds as if you were taken by surprise when you became pregnant. I'll state the obvious: when you have sex, you always increase the chances of becoming pregnant. The only person I know who got pregnant without sperm was Mary, Jesus' mother (see Luke 1:26-36).

I hear you taking some responsibility for becoming pregnant ("I made it, so I'm going to have to raise it."). Yet then you seem to blame God ("The Lord gave this to me for a reason, but I just don't know why.").

That makes me wonder, How did the Lord give this to you? The reason you became pregnant was that you had intercourse—not because the Lord was trying to give you something.

You mentioned that you considered having an abortion and decided not to. I want to say "Thank you!" When people are taken by surprise with a pregnancy, it usually seems as if all the options are bad ones. Yet you've chosen life in this situation, and that's a very good choice!

Becoming pregnant changes your life forever. It's a big thing—which also means sex is a big thing! In fact, it's bigger than most young people realize.

Here's some really good news, though: you're giving life to someone. It's a powerful experience!

Concerning your idea that God is trying to teach you something, I think God is always trying to teach us things. Your instruction will now come with an emphasis on being an awesome mom.

This may not be what you planned or expected. I'm certainly not going to blame God for your choices (and neither should you). But God can make something wonderful out of even our bad decisions.

Consider what Jesus did with His disciples. And you've probably seen what God can do today, too. He's eager to do something wonderful with your life and with the life of your developing child.

Here are some more encouraging passages for you: Isaiah 41:10; Jeremiah 33:3; Psalm 55:22; Romans 8:31-39; 2 Peter 1:3, 4; 2 Corinthians 5:17; Ephesians 3:20, 21; Psalm 68:19.

This may not be what you planned or expected. I'm certainly not going to blame God for your choices (and neither should you). But God can make something wonderful out of even our bad decisions.

What About Abortion?

ABORTION IS A TOPIC THAT CAN BE DEBATED— PEOPLE CAN ARGUE ONE SIDE OF THE ISSUE AS WELL AS THE OTHER.

Question: *What is the Seventh-day Adventist Church's stand on abortion? And please explain why.*

Answer: *Abortion is a topic that can be debated—people can argue one side of the issue as well as the other. But abortion becomes much less of a discussion topic when it is a life-and-death decision an individual is facing in real life.*

Whenever somebody asks me this question, first I want to find out if they're coming from an argumentative perspective (let's just hash it out and see who wins the argument), or if they're coming from the personal experience perspective (my best friend is thinking about having an *abortion, or I just had an abortion and I wonder if I really blew it!).*

Since you asked for "the Seventh-day Adventist Church's stand," I'm wondering who you think "the church" is. Some people think of a building as the church. In that case "the church" doesn't have any stand, because a building doesn't think. If you think of "the church" as the people who attend, then you'll get quite a variety of stands based on what each person thinks. My guess is that you're actually looking for an official statement from the denomination—the organized and elected church officers.

For years the official position of the Seventh-day Adventist Church on the topic of abortion was "there is no official position." Nobody had taken a strong enough stand or gathered enough group support to come up with an official position on abortion for the Seventh-day Adventist Church. The topic had been presented, argued, debated, written about, and more. But since there wasn't a clear consensus or direction, "the church" refused to make a stand.

People who opposed abortion thought it was horrible that the church wouldn't take a stand. And people in favor of abortion felt just as strongly the other way. In the meantime many people have decided whether or not to have an abortion without a clear statement from the Seventh-day Adventist Church.

The church's stand on abortion doesn't have to be so uncertain any longer. Anybody who has access to the Internet can find Seventh-day Adventist guidelines regarding abortion on www.adventist.org.

At the top left of the www.adventist.org home page you'll find a section called "Adventist Beliefs." Underneath "Adventist Beliefs" you'll find the section "Fundamental Beliefs." These are the basic beliefs of Adventism, such as the belief in God, in the Bible, etc. These are changed only during a General Conference session, and then after a very long process. The last time any changes were made to these beliefs was in 2005 and the most recent change prior to that was in 1980. You won't find "abortion" mentioned in the list of 28 Fundamental Beliefs, though. At this point it hasn't made it to "fundamental" status.

Two slots down is "Official Statements" of the Adventist Church. These aren't as basic as the "Fundamental Beliefs." However, they are topics that have significance, but on a secondary level of importance. These "statements" deal with issues that have come up which people are looking to "the church" to make a statement. These issues may have arisen at General Conference sessions (which take place every five years) or from other organizational meetings. In this section you'll find statements about the environment, AIDS, gambling, peace, homosexuality, racism, sexual abuse, homelessness, and many other topics. But abortion is not in this list.

The following section is called "Guidelines." In this section you'll find abortion to be the very first topic.

Here's a shortened version of seven guidelines given regarding abortion. But if you can, please go to the Web site and look up the full text version.

1. Prenatal human life is a magnificent gift of God.

2. Abortion is one of the tragic dilemmas of human fallenness.

3. In practical, tangible ways the Church as a supportive community should express its commitment to the value of human life.

4. The Church does not serve as conscience for individuals; however, it should provide moral guidance.

5. Christians acknowledge as first and foremost their accountability to God.

6. Church institutions should be provided with guidelines for developing their own institutional policies in harmony with this statement.

7. Church members should be encouraged to participate in the ongoing consideration of their moral responsibilities with regard to abortion in light of the teaching of Scripture.

What does all of this mean? First of all it means that the Seventh-day Adventist Church is moving toward an official statement on the topic of abortion. The date of this "Guideline" is October 12, 1992, which is probably before you were born.

It also means that the Seventh-day Adventist Church sees life as a gift from God, including life growing in the uterus of a woman—"prenatal life." The Church also recognizes that abortion isn't an easy decision; one that's been complicated by sin in our world and in our lives. The official position of the Seventh-day Adventist Church is to help people, including those who face the issue of abortion. However, the church will not dictate that a person should or shouldn't have an abortion.

But what if a person is actually having to decide whether or not to have an abortion? Instead of just talking about it or arguing in a group, when a person has an "unwanted pregnancy," several issues come up such as:

- Why did this happen?

- Who is the father? (Sometimes a person isn't sure.)

- What will happen if I keep the baby?

- What will happen to the baby and to me if I allow someone else to adopt the baby?

- If I have an abortion, will I be guilty of murder?

When a person faces an unwanted pregnancy, all the options look bad. It's too late to say, "Don't have sex" or "I told you so!" Our culture promotes such a double standard; it condones sexual activity, then debates whether or not to abort its result.

Just as intercourse is more than a physical act, the development of a baby over a nine-month period is much more than physical development. A tremendous amount of emotional bonding with the baby-in-formation occurs with the mother and with the father, too! No wonder it's a complicated issue.

Let's say a young lady, we'll call her Becka, is in her teens or early 20s, and she finds out that she's pregnant. She didn't want to get pregnant. Many variables will influence Becka's decision as to what to do.

Is Becka excited? embarrassed? angry? resigned? afraid? hopeful? hopeless? What about the father? Is he supportive? forceful? demanding? responsible? flakey? angry? blaming? available? Will the soon-to-be-parents get married? What support systems do they have to rely on? Are there family members who can help? Is there church family to offer support? Are there friends who'll offer presence and encouragement?

Because most churches teach that sex is for marriage, a pregnancy outside of marriage provides ample proof that a couple hasn't followed the church's teachings. So why would Becka (and the father) consider church teachings when it comes to abortion?

Will Becka have an abortion out of guilt? Will she get the cold shoulder (or feel like she's getting it) from church members? Will she avoid church all together?

The arguments about when life begins—at conception, after the first, second, or third trimester of pregnancy—can be debated. But when a person actually becomes pregnant, the emotional, social, and hormonal elements impact the abortion decision well beyond a simple "yes" or "no."

If Becka decides to carry the baby to term, but the father suggests an abortion because "they both still need to complete college," and church members are talking behind her back, how might those situations impact Becka's decision?

What if two weeks later Becka isn't so sure about carrying the baby to term; the father demands an abortion, or he'll leave the state; other family members are encouraging an abortion; and church members freely share with each other that it looks like Becka is making another disastrous choice after her sinful choice? What will Becka do then? My guess is that she'll be more likely to have an abortion and not be part of church life anymore.

You can say, "Abortion is wrong!" But how will you treat someone like Becka who considers an abortion or follows through with one? Or what will you think of her, and how will you treat her if she has the baby?

I'm grateful there are adoption agencies, such as the Adventist-based adoption service called Christian Family Adoption, that provide a wonderful option of carrying the baby to term and giving the baby to people who are ready and eager to have a family.

The Seventh-day Adventist Church promotes life and recognizes that abortion exists because our world is a mess. The organized and elected church officers have called all Seventh-day Adventist Churches to be supportive of a person with an unwanted pregnancy, so abortion isn't their decision of preference. Now, that doesn't guarantee your church will be supportive, just like there isn't a guarantee that no teen in any Adventist Church will ever have an unwanted pregnancy.

Deciding how to handle an unwanted pregnancy isn't easy. Each of these three options has negative consequences:

1. Abortion eliminates the growing life, and God is for life, not its elimination. Often there are also emotional damages that exceed any physical ones.

2. Babies change people's lives more than marriage does. Some question the quality of life for the child that results from an unwanted pregnancy. Will the child have two parents? What kind of financial pressures is the child destined to encounter? Who will be "family"?

3. Giving the baby up for adoption preserves the life of the growing fetus. It also provides a life for those who aren't creating life for whatever reason. However, the baby's biological mother is apt to wonder what would've happened if she would've kept the baby.

I know it's a difficult choice, but I'd recommend the third option—giving the baby up for adoption. It promotes life, recognizes difficulties, honors personal choice, and provides a second chance for the mom, dad, baby, and the couple who'll finally have a child.

What About Dancing— Is It Wrong?

"WE PLAYED THE FLUTE FOR YOU, AND YOU DID NOT DANCE; WE SANG A DIRGE, AND YOU DID NOT MOURN."

(MATTHEW 11:16, 17)

Question: *When my friends and I have parties, we usually dance. It never leads to anything, and I don't think about it afterward. Do you think it's wrong to dance?*

Answer: *Dancing can certainly provoke a heated discussion. I'm discovering that in youth group debates some people consider it a "no-no," but other people "just do it" anyway.*

What has God told us about dancing? That matters more than what people say in church, or what people do on their own time.

Years ago I edited a book called *Shall We Dance.* It includes biblical principles for a number of lifestyle issues, including dancing. Here are the key principles and passages on the topic of dancing that I discovered:

264

1. Dance is a component of divine worship (see 2 Samuel 6:14; 1 Chronicles 15:29; Psalm 149:3; and Psalm 150:4).

2. Dance is an appropriate expression of community joy (see Judges 11:34; 1 Samuel 18:6; Matthew 11:17; Luke 7:32; and Luke 15:25).

3. Dance should praise no other god but God/Yahweh (see the golden calf story in Exodus 32).

4. Dance should not promote inappropriate sexual arousal (see 1 Corinthians 10:7, 8 and Matthew 14:6).

5. Appropriate dance is dance in which God is invited as a witness and participant (see 1 Corinthians 10:31 and Romans 14:23).

The concern people express in religious circles usually relates to principle 4—inappropriate sexual arousal. But in your question you seem to indicate that that's not an issue—although it doesn't seem that the parties you refer to are times of worship (referring to principles 1 and 3).

That means that principles 2 and 5 apply directly to your situation. I'm guessing that your party is similar to a time of celebrating community joy, although your party "community" is probably rather small. Perhaps the most important question for you to answer is whether or not God is at your party as a witness and as a participant.

You asked me if I thought it's wrong to dance. Although you'd have to be a fool to think that dancing would never be a problem for Christians, perhaps we've missed out on appropriate dancing by categorizing all dance as evil.

It was Jesus who said, "To what can I compare this generation? They are like children sitting in the marketplaces and calling out to others:

'We played the flute for you,
and you did not dance;
we sang a dirge,
and you did not mourn'" (Matthew 11:16, 17).

I think it would be good to do more Christian celebrating and have more joyful expression instead of living as if Christianity is devoid of all fun.

What About Makeup?

"WHEN JEZEBEL,
THE QUEEN
MOTHER, HEARD
THAT JEHU HAD
COME TO JEZREEL,
SHE PAINTED HER
EYELIDS AND
FIXED HER HAIR
AND SAT AT A
WINDOW."

2 KINGS 9:30 (NLT)

Question: *How do you think God feels about makeup? Does wearing makeup mean I don't think God made me pretty enough, even if I don't overdo it? Does God not want me to wear makeup, and am I sinning if I do?*

Answer: *Someone asked a famous Seventh-day Adventist minister this same kind of question—Is it wrong to wear makeup? His answer was "If the fence needs painting, then paint it!"*

The Bible doesn't say much about makeup. Most people would agree that makeup fits into a larger category of outward appearance, including how we dress and how we adorn ourselves (jewelry *and other "acceptable" Adventist items like neckties, scarves, pins, and Pathfinder paraphernalia).*

One text that some use is 2 Kings 9:30: "When Jezebel, the queen mother, heard that Jehu had come to Jezreel, she painted her eyelids and fixed her hair and sat at a window" (NLT). If you read the whole story, you'll discover that it's not about painting eyelids. Wicked queen Jezebel's son, King Joram, had just been killed by Jehu.

Jezebel decked herself out and called down from the window to ask if Jehu had come in peace or not. Jehu reported that he hadn't, and several people near the window ended up pushing Jezebel out the window to her death below. So I guess makeup on the eyes isn't as useful as a parachute at times.

By associating wicked Queen Jezebel with painting one's eyes, some think that if a person uses eyeliner or eye shadow, that person will become a Jezebel. But Jezebel also fixed her hair and sat at a window. Are these equally as sinful?

Two other passages that refer to some type of makeup are Jeremiah 4:30 and Ezekiel 23:40. Jeremiah 4:30 says, "What are you doing, you who have been plundered? Why do you dress up in your most beautiful clothing and jewelry? Why do you brighten your eyes with mascara? It will do you no good! Your allies despise you and will kill you" (Jeremiah 4:30, NLT).

Ezekiel 23:40 says, "You sisters sent messengers to distant lands to get men. Then when they arrived, you bathed yourselves, painted your eyelids, and put on your finest jewels for them" (NLT).

The stories in both passages are similar. God is married to His people, but His people primp themselves not for God, but to go after other lovers instead of God. Makeup is not the issue—unfaithfulness to God is the issue.

If you apply this to yourself and how you dress, ask yourself, "Why do I dress the way I do?" and "Why do I accessorize the way I do?" and "Why do I want to look nice?"

Usually people dress nice so others will see them as nice-looking. Some think baggy clothes are nice, while others prefer tightly fitting clothes. Compare how adults dress to how teens dress. Both generations think they dress nice, and the other generation doesn't.

Makeup usually is a female thing more than a male thing. As a male, I don't understand why girls put on makeup to look "natural." A number of times my wife has tried to explain that looking "natural" means using makeup to give your face an even look instead of a splotchy look.

Unnatural makeup is usually a bold color, which makes lips or eyes or other parts of your face stand out and get noticed more than usual. I suppose that a flashing neon light around one's face could do the same thing.

Let's rephrase your question from "What's wrong with makeup?" to "What's wrong with looking nice?" For those who think that looking nice is sinful and looking ugly is spiritual—you're wrong! Looking ugly isn't spiritual; it's just ugly! And some would argue that looking nice is the way to go because after all, we're created in God's image (Genesis 1:27).

It's quite common for people of all ages to want others who matter to them to think they are nice-looking. Outward physical beauty is what people notice first, before your inner, character-quality beauty. But after the first impression, outward beauty goes down in value while inner beauty continues to climb.

So be absolutely beautiful! Develop your inner beauty so that it's more beautiful than your outward beauty. Otherwise, an outward beauty without an inner beauty is like a gold ring hanging in a pig's snout (see Proverbs 11:22).

Here's how Peter put it: "You should not use outward aids to make yourselves beautiful, such as the way you fix your hair, or the jewelry you put on, or the dresses you wear. Instead, your inner beauty should consist of your true inner self, the ageless beauty of a gentle and quiet spirit, which is of the greatest value in God's sight" (1 Peter 3:3, 4, TEV). This doesn't mean it's a sin to look beautiful. It's a sin when your outward looks are more beautiful than your character. That's false advertising!

Keep in mind that there will always be suckers who are satisfied with outer beauty alone, as well as insecure females who will spend more attention on their outward appearance than on their character and even their personality.

What do people notice about you? What makes you nice-looking?

Keep in mind that there will always be suckers who are satisfied with outer beauty alone, as well as insecure females who will spend more attention on their outward appearance than on their character and even their personality.

What About Graduations on Sabbath?

No matter how much of a "victim" you are because of the choice of others, you often still retain a certain amount of choice for yourself.

Question: *My high school graduation is on Sabbath. I didn't make the decision on when it would be, so it would be okay to go, wouldn't it? But something is telling me it's not right. Would I be compromising my faith if I went to my graduation? What are the pro's and con's? I want to make the right choice.*

Answer: *I wish more people would take their faith seriously and ask themselves how their decisions will impact their relationship with God. I admire you for doing so.*

W*hile you are learning to make all kinds of choices on your own, there are* *still some that you don't get to choose (like which day of the week graduation will be held). In case you're wondering, there will always be decisions made beyond your control. When you're all done with school, similar situations will arise about your work (such as when the company picnic will be, whether or not alcohol will be served at the Christmas party, the temporary favoritism the boss shows to the person who's having sex with him, etc.). No matter how much of a "victim" you are because of the choice of others, you often still retain a certain amount of choice for yourself (Will I be part of the company picnic? Will I drink alcohol at the Christmas party or leave when things start going downhill? Will I give myself away sexually to be part of that power game of use and abuse? etc.).*

You mentioned, "But something is telling me it's not right." I'd strongly recommend that you spend some time focusing on that impression. Where is it coming from? Usually God communicates in a quiet voice rather than through shouting. You don't want to drown out the "still, small voice." But you should certainly ask yourself where that message has its root. Is it something you've always heard and never questioned? Is it just a habit? Is it something that came from your reading of Scripture or while you were listening to God during a time of prayer? Is this message coming from God, from others, or who knows where? By all means, take this issue back to God in prayer and ask for Him to send you an answer!

I like your suggestion of making a list of pro's and con's. That's usually a good step to take in making decisions. Not every item on the list carries the same weight. In other words, you might have eight items on the con list and only three on the pro list, but something on the pro side might carry more weight (be more important) than everything on the other side combined!

Let me start a pro and con list for you, and then why don't you complete it, okay?

Pro's and Con's of going to my high school graduation on Sabbath

PRO's

1. Celebrate the culmination of all my high school years of school

2. Be present with my class at this crowning event

3. Publicly accept the reward my school is giving to me

4. Have stories and memories for the rest of my life

5.

6.

7.

CON's

1. Participate in a secular event during the Sabbath

2. Make an exception to my Sabbath commitment

3. Potentially compromise my witness

4. Not worship with my congregation for one Sabbath

5.

6.

7.

You asked what I would do if I were faced with your situation. I attended an Adventist academy, so we actually had three graduation services on graduation weekend. Two of the three were during the Sabbath hours. On Friday night we had a consecration service which was intended as a time for us to prepare ourselves and then commit ourselves to God. On Sabbath morning, our regular church service got adapted to include a processional and then the sermon was geared specifically for the graduates. It was called the Baccalaureate service, which is the preaching portion of a graduation—appropriate for church time. On Sunday, we had the graduation commencement where the diplomas and awards got handed out. The first two services were held in a church. The last service was held at the school.

Since I didn't attend a public high school, I can tell you what I'd do only by using my imagination. Because I see a high school graduation as a celebration of an achievement that God has made in me and through me, I think I would go to the graduation ceremony. I think the festivities of the day can be consistent with the celebration our Creator initiated for the first Sabbath. I'd take God with me to graduation rather than leaving Him at the church. According to the fourth commandment (see Exodus 20:8-11) the Sabbath is a day to remember what God has done rather than a day of just regular work. I wouldn't put graduation in the same category of just another day of school. I wouldn't consider my graduation to be something God couldn't attend, even if in a public sphere (in America) there is an attempt to keep God and schools separate.

I don't know what time of day your graduation service will take place, but I think I'd arrange for a gathering of family and church members to celebrate and consecrate me at this high moment called graduation. If there were others in my church graduating around this same time (8th grade, high school or college), I suggest making them part of the celebration, too. I'd probably do that rather than go to the other graduation parties because I don't think they would have the same religious character that would be appropriate for Sabbath.

Now, just because I think that's what I'd do doesn't mean that you should do it. Please notice my reasons and not just my actions. It's important to consider the motivations and purposes for what you do, not just what you do.

I'd talk it over with my family, including my church family, and get their input in addition to my times communing with God. I'd talk to a teacher or administrator at my school and get their input as well. I'd keep it a matter of prayer until I received peace about it, and then I'd proceed with the decision that brought about peace.

Congratulations! And now what?

What About Competing on Sabbath?

CLEARLY SABBATH IS A DAY DEDICATED TO GOD. SO IF YOU CHOOSE TO DO YOUR OWN THING—AND YOU CAN CERTAINLY CHOOSE TO DO THAT—YOU TOTALLY IGNORE THE WHOLE IDEA OF DEDICATING THE DAY TO THE ONE WHO MADE YOU, INCLUDING YOUR ABILITY TO SWIM.

Question: *I'm on a swimming team, and we're going to a big swimming meet in another country to compete against 32 countries! The meet will be on Sabbath and Sunday. I will compete only on Sunday. But what should I do on Sabbath while everyone else is at the meet? Would it be wrong if I competed on Sabbath?*

Answer: *Congratulations on qualifying to go! But what should you do when you really want to keep Sabbath holy and swim at the big swimming meet?*

Let's look at the Sabbath commandment from Exodus 20:8-11: "Remember the Sabbath day by keeping it *holy. Six days you shall labor and do all your work, but the seventh day is a Sabbath to the Lord your God. On it you shall not do any work, neither you, nor your son or daughter, nor your manservant or maidservant, nor your animals, nor the alien within your gates. For in six days the Lord made the heavens and the earth, the sea, and all that is in them, but he rested on the seventh day. Therefore the Lord blessed the Sabbath day and made it holy."*

Clearly Sabbath is a day dedicated to God. So if you choose to do your own thing—and you can certainly choose to do that—you totally ignore the whole idea of dedicating the day to the One who made you, including your ability to swim.

Is there anything more important to you than swimming in that meet? If your answer is no, then you've just revealed that swimming in the meet is your god—the most important thing in your life.

If your answer is yes, then God is more important to you than swimming in the meet. And you'll want to hang with God on that special day to focus on Him.

If God isn't more important to you than swimming, but you'd like for Him to be, then choose Him over swimming. If you do, your value for God and His Sabbath will increase.

Think about this comparison. This swimming meet is important because 32 countries will be there, and it happens only once in a while—maybe once in your life, unless you end up going to the Olympics. The Sabbath is important because God is the Creator of all the countries, and He makes Sabbath happen again and again. So why refuse this gift from your Creator?

If you haven't seen *Chariots of Fire*, I recommend that you rent it at a video store. It's old, but the character in the story faces your same dilemma. Check it out. I hope your ending will be similar to his!

What could you do on Sabbath while your teammates are competing? Look for a church near the place of competition. You could check out God's creation in that setting, even listen to some of your favorite Christian music. Try hooking up with some other Adventist friends, if possible, and laugh a lot.

Do something active rather than just sit and think about the meet. Then spend time in prayer and continue long enough to start listening to God instead of only talking to Him. It could be the best Sabbath of your life so far!

If God isn't more important to you than swimming, but you'd like for Him to be, then choose Him over swimming. If you do, your value for God and His Sabbath will increase.

What About Cussing?

I'VE NOTICED THAT SOME PEOPLE CUSS AS A WAY TO "BE COOL." IT GETS ATTENTION AND SHOWS DISDAIN FOR AUTHORITY FIGURES WHO DISAPPROVE OF VULGAR LANGUAGE.

Question: *Is cussing a sin? I don't see it in the Bible.*

Answer: *Cussing is a form of swearing. When people use a cussword, it's usually to express something negative. Every language has its own cusswords. Typically they have something to do with sexuality (private body parts, crude intercourse, or excrement/waste) or condemnation (sometimes calling out to God to do it).*

I*'ve noticed that some people cuss as a way to "be cool." It gets attention and shows disdain for authority figures who disapprove of vulgar language.*

When I was young I went through a period of wanting people to think of me as something apart from a "goody-goody Christian." So I learned a few cusswords and used them in nearly every sentence. After a short time people no longer thought of me as a Christian.

The reason people don't associate a foul mouth with Christianity is found in Galatians 5:16-26. Verse 16 reads, "I advise you to live according to your new life in the Holy Spirit. Then you won't be doing what your sinful nature craves."

Another form of "swearing" is to condemn something, often calling for God to do it. Instead of saying it directly to his enemies, David poured out his anguish to God. Check out these verses from Psalm 69.

Verse 24 says, "Pour out your fury on them; consume them with your burning anger." Verse 27 says, "Pile their sins up high, and don't let them go free." Verse 28 says, "Erase their names from the Book of Life; don't let them be counted among the righteous."

When talking about swearing, often people appeal to the third commandment: "Do not misuse the name of the Lord your God. The Lord will not let you go unpunished if you misuse his name" (Exodus 20:7).

How do you misuse God's name? Some think it's using swear phrases, such as "Oh, my God" or "Oh God" or "God," or saying with disgust or exasperation, "Jesus Christ." Others think it means being a Christian, but being a hypocrite about it.

Another form of swearing is people making a statement and adding, "I swear." Jesus warned against this. He said, "Just say a simple, 'Yes, I will,' or 'No, I won't.' Your word is enough. To strengthen your promise with a vow shows that something is wrong" (Matthew 5:37).

You asked if cussing was a sin and about whether or not it's in the Bible. It can be vulgar and in poor taste. And yes, it's in the Bible. David seemed to do it in releasing anger and pain to God instead of to others. But Jesus said to use simple speech rather than adding more emphasis through swearing.

If you're in the habit of cussing or swearing and want to break it, you can. Praying puts you in touch with supernatural power. Enlarging your vocabulary is a way to build an arsenal for articulating your perspective. And holding your tongue before repeating filthy words enables you to come up with more wholesome phrases so you won't need to cuss or swear.

Praying puts you in touch with supernatural power. Enlarging your vocabulary is a way to build an arsenal for articulating your perspective. And holding your tongue before repeating filthy words enables you to come up with more wholesome phrases so you won't need to cuss or swear.

What About Getting Money for a Mission Trip?

SO MANY PEOPLE HAVE HAD SUCH POSITIVE SPIRITUAL GROWTH EXPERIENCES BY GOING ON A SHORT-TERM MISSION TRIP (FOR ONE TO TWO WEEKS) OR BY BEING A STUDENT MISSIONARY (FOR A YEAR).

Question: *I'm starting to save money for a mission trip. Any advice for me?*

Answer: *Yes, but first I want to say, "Way to go!" So many people have had such positive spiritual growth experiences by going on a short-term mission trip (for one to two weeks) or by being a student missionary (for a year).*

Yes, *mission trips are expensive! The most expensive item usually is your travel (often $500-$1,000, or even $2,000 if you go halfway around the world). Your expenses for food, shelter, ground transportation, construction materials, evangelistic supplies, insurance, etc., often* *come to $300-$600. So it could cost you $800-$1,600 ($2,500-$3,000 halfway around the world). Student missionaries usually have to raise $2,000-$2,500 for airfare to their destination.*

When a school or church goes on a short-term mission trip, lots of people get involved raising money. Everyone going on the trip may ask the same people for financial assistance, so the funding gets a bit thin.

For a short-term mission trip such as the Ultimate Workout (www.ultimateworkout.org) or a student missionary stint, it's usually one person from a church going. That one person can be the "real-life missionary" for the local church.

Don't try to go it alone simply by baking and selling cookies or by auctioning off your siblings as slaves. It is wise to also invite the church members to help sponsor you for $10, $25, or even $50 or $100.

Some young people hesitate to ask because they feel as if they're begging for money. Change your mind-set. Instead of begging for money, you're inviting church members to join your team as a sponsor for missions. Of course, you'll need to keep your sponsors up-to-date on how things develop, as well as reporting to them when you get back.

You can also ask out-of-town relatives and friends to sponsor you. And when people ask you for gift ideas at Christmastime, birthdays, or graduation, tell them to put funds toward your mission trip instead.

I often tell young people to pray for God to work a miracle if He wants them to go. And then I advise them to make a whole bunch of contacts by phone, letters, e-mails, and in person.

If no doors open (no sponsorships by the deadline), then you should ask God to show you where else He wants you to serve. If God wants you to go, the way will be prepared.

Each year I hear incredible stories of people who didn't expect to go on the Ultimate Workout, but then the miracles started to happen. If those miracles don't happen, then use that time to do a local mission trip in your own community, or a less-expensive "mission trip" in your own country.

Also, remember that raising money is just one part of preparing for a mission trip. More importantly, you need to prepare your heart, mind, and attitude. Ask God to transform you into whatever He wants you to be in this cross-cultural mission experience.

Also, remember that raising money is just one part of preparing for a mission trip. More importantly, you need to prepare your heart, mind, and attitude. Ask God to transform you into whatever He wants you to be in this cross-cultural mission experience.

Scripture Index

287